Praise

"I've loved this book for sixty years. My first copy was borrowed from the Philadelphia Public Library when I was fourteen, and I kept renewing the loan till I could afford to own my own copy. *Houdini's Fabulous Magic* has just the right blend of history, technical secrets, and romance to fire the passion of a young magician. Four pieces of the Penn & Teller repertoire were directly inspired by *Houdini's Fabulous Magic*—four times more than any other book in my library."

TELLER OF PENN & TELLER

Foreword by
Gabe Fajuri

HOUDINI'S FABULOUS MAGIC

WALTER R. GIBSON
AND MORRIS N. YOUNG

www.vineleavespress.com

Print Edition, 1st Edition in this form
ISBN: 978-618-86077-8-1
Published by Vine Leaves Press in Greece 2022
First printed in Philadelphia by Chilton Company and in Toronto by Ambassadors Books, Ltd. in 1961

Acknowledgment is made to Harcourt, Brace & World, Inc., for permission to reproduce herein : (a) Figs. 19, 22-27, 29, 32, 43, 44, 46, and 47 from Houdini's Escapes, by Walter B. Gibson, copyright 1930 by Bernard M. L. Ernst; renewed 1958 by Rob-erta C. Ernst; (b) Fig. 45 from Houdini's Magic, by Walter B. Gibson, copyright 1932 by Bernard M. L. Ernst; renewed 1960 by Roberta C. Ernst.

Cover design by Jessica Bell
Interior design by Amie McCracken

A catalogue record of this work is available from The National Library of Greece.

Table of Contents

Harry Houdini

Foreword

DISSECTING HOUDINI'S LIFE, his career, and the meaning of it all is a subject of endless fascination. No other magician has captured the public's interest so completely or enduringly.

In the decades since his demise, the stories analyzing Houdini's life, his deeds, his upbringing, his family, and his career have been produced in a steady and unending stream, on film and stage, in print, and every other medium known to mankind. "The Master Mystifier's" appeal is, it seems, timeless.

Morris Young and Walter Gibson, a seemingly unlikely set of collaborators, stepped back into the Houdiniverse in 1961 when their work—this book—*Houdini's Fabulous Magic*, was first published.

By then, Young, an Ophthalmologist by trade, had donated his impressive collection of Houdiniana to the Library of Congress, where it joined much of the great magician's own library, collection, and personal papers.

Young was an early and ardent champion of the Houdini legend, and approached his subject from the perspective of not just a fan, but a trained and thoughtful academic. As a boy growing up in Massachusetts he was enchanted by conjuring in all its facets and its lifelong hold on his intellect was firmly set when he met Houdini in person.

In the decades that followed, and particularly after Houdini's unexpected and untimely death in 1926, Young collected and collated much of the ephemera and archival material that helped tell Houdini's story and build his legend.

A writer by trade but always a magician at heart, Walter Gibson was the twentieth century's great literary ghost for all things magic-related. And by the time *Houdini's Fabulous Magic* saw print, he had been knee-deep in the escape artist's world for over thirty years. In fact, he had collaborated with Houdini as a ghostwriter, just as he did with nearly every other famous magician of the "golden age" of the art.

After Houdini's death, Gibson wrote two books about the magician and his work based on Houdini's own notebooks and detailing the methods behind many (but not all) of his famous escapes and tricks.

In 1953, through a shared fascination and friendship bound by their love for the subject matter, the two men collaborated on their first book of Houdiniana, a work that revealed some of the master magician's secrets, *Houdini on Magic*. It became a popular source to answer the never-ending question on the minds and mouths of nearly everyone who has ever witnessed a conjuring trick: how did he do it?

Houdini's Fabulous Magic continued answering that question, as this work, like its predecessor, gives readers a behind the curtain peek at the secrets that helped build Houdini's reputation.

While many a magician would contend that explaining a magic trick is a bit like explaining a joke (in other words, painfully boring), this writer is decidedly not in that camp. Nor were, I suspect, Gibson and Young. As their text reveals, the ingenuity required to accomplish many of Houdini's greatest feats—and the more modest ones, too—was considerable.

And yet I would not recommend anyone thumbing through the pages that follow, or thrilling to the discovery of the secrets behind some of Houdini's most famous escapes, actually go out and attempt an overboard packing box escape, encase himself in a canvas mail bag, get locked in a jail cell (for any reason), or construct a Water Torture Cell or galvanized Milk Can, no matter what method of escape is planned. As Gibson and Young explain, the appeal of many of these stunts is their inherent danger.

On the contrary, I can wholeheartedly recommend developing an understanding of the methods behind what Houdini did as a jumping off point for further study.

There is a certain level of genius (an often-overused word, I know) behind these feats of wonderment. How does one make the impossible a practical, performable reality? Ingenuity, as Gibson and Young reveal, will take you part of the way there.

There are also, as you will discover, mechanical devices, living pachyderms, corps of trained assistants, and a healthy dose of guts and determination required to success-fully perform many of these miracles.

The other elements required, which peek through the pages of *Houdini's Fabulous Magic* from time to time, were publicity and showmanship. And these elements no expla-nation of a Vanishing Elephant can truly encapsulate or fully explain.

There are many reasons Houdini's name remains on the lips and minds of the public some 100 years after his passing, and while some may argue that first and foremost it was his daring escapes that made his legacy so enduring, without showmanship and publicity those feats would not have endured.

Certainly there were others who escaped from handcuffs before Houdini, as did other entertainers imitate his most remarkable escapes. But it was Houdini who exploited these performances, these jail breaks, and even said Vanishing Elephant—which by some accounts, was more publicity stunt than theatrical miracle—to their fullest extent.

Houdini gathered crowds of thousands to watch him jump, manacled and bound, into one river after another. It was his way to dramatize these feats. After tense moments passed, he bobbed to the surface, having escaped both his metal bonds and certain death. Likewise, vast throngs watched him wriggle free of straitjackets while suspended from a rope by his ankles high above city streets.

Gibson and Young make all these elements clear in the pages that follow, teasing at some, diving deep into others, and inviting further inquiry from the truly engaged. So if your goal is to understand, at least from an armchair perspective, what it took to make the magic work as well as what it took to make it spectacular, read on.

As you turn each page, you'll gain a rarefied view into the secret world of a great magician, a man who was arguably the world's greatest.

It's a perspective that only those who know where to look are able to see.

Gabe Fajuri is a publisher, author, editor, and auctioneer, who in a career spanning three decades has discovered, researched, cataloged, and written about countless Houdini relics, from escape devices, handcuffs, and magic props used in Houdini's performances, to rare troves of documents, family heirlooms, and related memorabilia. He lives in Chicago.

The Substitution Trunk

WHEN HARRY and Bessie Houdini went on the road as a team in 1894, playing beer halls and dime museums, they featured a trick billed as "Metamorphosis" and which they also claimed to be "The Greatest Novelty Mystery Act in the World!"

The description of this wonder stated:

> Mons. Houdini's hands are fastened behind his back, he is securely tied in a bag and the knots are sealed, then placed in a massive box which is locked and sealed. The box is then rolled into a small cabinet and Mlle. Houdini draws the curtain and claps her hand three times. At the last clap of her hands the curtain is drawn open by Mons. Houdini and Mlle. Houdini has disappeared. Upon the box being opened, she is found in his place in the bag, the seals unbroken and her hands tied in precisely the same manner as were Mons. Houdini's when first entering the bag *Just think this over: the time consumed in making the change is THREE SECONDS!*

All the Apparatus used in this Act is inspected by a Committee selected from the Audience.

We challenge the World to produce an act done with greater Mystery, Speed or Dexterity.

It was this act that gained the Houdinis their engagement with the Welsh Brothers Circus in 1895 and again in 1898 as testified in a letter from the circus management:

We can cheerfully recommend Harry and Beatrice Houdini with their unique and mysterious act called "Metamorphosis" as being the strongest drawing card of its class in America. Their act is totally unlike others and always creates a profound impression upon their auditors.

Fig. 2

Two significant points should be noted in the description of this act; namely, that the trunk was described as a box and that Houdini's hands were tied behind him. After the Houdinis went into vaudeville and Harry became famous for his "Handcuff Act," the trunk was more widely recognized, though it was still loosely termed a "Box Trick" as witness this description of Houdini's performance at the Alhambra Theatre in London, during his return engagement in December 1900:

Houdini concludes his show with an exceptionally smart Box Trick in which he is ably assisted by Mrs. Houdini, whose untiring efforts to secure the maximum of effect are very apparent. Houdini, wearing a borrowed coat, and with hands tied behind, steps into an examined sack, which, duly tied and sealed, is placed in one of those beautiful large trunks which Americans are so fond of bringing over here to knock spots off our hotel porters.

The trunk is locked and corded and placed in a large curtained enclosure. Mrs. Houdini now exclaims, "I will step into the cabinet and clap my hands three times—then notice the effect." The lady has barely had time to do as stated when Houdini rushes out minus coat and free. The box is next pulled out and opened, when Mrs. Houdini is found inside the bag, seals of which are intact, wearing the borrowed coat and with hands tied behind her back.

The actual "change" takes from three to five seconds and it is obtained without the aid of duplicity, change of costume or of concealed stage appliances and on a stage not absolutely set apart for Magical Productions.

The final paragraph is particularly important, as will be seen when we come to an explanation of the trick. It was included for the benefit of magical readers, as the review appeared in Stanyon's *Magic* for 1901 whose circulation was among members of the trade.

Skipping on through the years, we find this brief but glowing account of the same Trunk Trick, written by a witness whom Houdini personally invited on the stage to serve as a member of the committee.

This was on June 2, 1922, in New York City, and the witness stated:

> Houdini gave a perfectly amazing performance, in which having been packed into a bag and the bag into a trunk, corded up and locked, he was out again after only a few seconds' concealment in a tent, while in his place his wife was found, equally bound, bagged and boxed, with my dress-coat on which I had put upon him before I tied his hands behind him. Houdini is the greatest conjurer in the world and this is his greatest trick.

That was written by Sir Arthur Conan Doyle, the creator of Sherlock Holmes, who was a guest of honor at a magicians' banquet held at the Hotel McAlpin in New York. The description is quoted from his book, *Our American Adventure,* which was published a year later.

It will be noted that no change had been made in the presentation of the "Substitution Trunk," as the trick had come to be called, during the twenty-odd years between the Stanyon review and the Doyle report. Actually, the 1922 presentation was something of a revival of "Metamorphosis" which the Houdinis had shown only at intervals. Houdini had worked his "Milk Can" and the "Chinese Water Torture Cell" as well as many other escapes as a "single" act in which Bessie had not participated.

But soon after the New York event, they took out the Substitution Trunk again and after touring with it in vaudeville, used it in the full evening show which Houdini was presenting at the time of his death. So Conan Doyle was indeed right in one sense, when he classed it as Houdini's "greatest trick," for it was the sensational feature with which Houdini began and ended his career.

The original "Box Trick" was presented by John Nevil Maskelyne in England, on June 19, 1865, when he escaped from a locked and corded wooden box to prove that he could outdo the "manifestations" of the Davenport Brothers, a pair of pretended spirit mediums. The trick was so successful that Maskelyne continued to show it in one form or another over many years.

Rivals sprang up, due to Maskelyne's offer of a reward to anyone who could solve the secret. Other performers duplicated the feat, but Maskelyne insisted that their methods were not the same as the original.

Whatever the case, by the 1890s, the Box Trick had become a stage illusion, and in one version, the performer disappeared from one trunk and reappeared in another. But this required either "concealed stage appliances" or a "special stage" as Stanyon would have termed it.

In another version, known as "The Indian Mail," only the trunk was needed. The magician was placed in a sack, which in turn was locked in a box or trunk from which he made his escape, stepping into sight from behind the screens that hid the trunk and bringing the sack with him.

The magician then returned behind the screens which were removed by assistants to show the magician gone. The trunk was opened, and he was found still tied within the sack. An illusion of this type was featured by Herrmann the Great as the "Asiatic Trunk Mystery," which he billed as his "Original Oriental Sensation." Herrmann was making an entire act of it in the full evening show that he was presenting at the time of his death in 1896.

Other magicians were doing Box Tricks, one even being titled "The Packer's Surprise," but the effect often lacked impact for two reasons:

If done as an escape, the opening of the box to show it empty was something of an anticlimax, as the trick was all over.

If the magician himself returned to the box and was found there, many audiences would think in terms of "doubles" and claim that the performer had simply let someone pose for him outside the box.

Both of those objections were overcome by turning the illusion into a "quick change" or "transformation" and from that idea "Metamorphosis" was born, both as a trick and a title. Houdini worked the Box Trick with his partner Hayman as the "Houdini Brothers" and later he used his own brother Theo, called Hardeen, in the same act.

But it still was just a "good trick" rather than a "sensational mystery" because the performers looked too much alike, particularly the real brothers, Harry and Theo, who could actually double for each other. It was when Harry and Bessie became the "Houdinis" that they left their audiences totally amazed by the Substitution Trunk.

The "change" of a man for a woman, apparently in a matter of a few seconds, was a startling surprise that held the audience in real suspense until they were provided with the real "convincer": they saw the very person in the trunk who had been on full view up to a few moments before the original prisoner had stepped out free.

In a word, the Substitution Trunk became one hundred percent effect, with method playing an almost separate part. It was so astounding that audiences would have been overwhelmed even if trunk and sack had been only casually shown; but to subject those items to the scrutiny of a committee made the riddle all the stronger.

Like every riddle, this one had an answer. It is given in the following explanation, which has been checked with contemporary accounts (around 1900) that covered the trick very much as the Houdinis performed it.

First, as to the tying of the wrists, Houdini was adept with rope and tape ties, including those in which the knots could be "slipped" and tightened later. He released himself from the rope while the sack was being pulled up over his head, so he was free to operate further and immediately.

The next operation concerned the sack. In one type of sack the cord ran through metal eyelets around the upper edge a few inches apart, so the rope would be alternately inside and outside. A grip on an inside portion enables the performer to pull it down into a long interior loop. After the ends of the cord are tied and the knots sealed, the sack can still be opened sufficiently for a quick escape.

The trunk was a very large one, allowing freedom of movement inside it. It had a rear panel opening inward, with a secret release on the inside. Houdini was out of the sack and coat by the time the trunk was locked and roped. As soon as the trunk was hidden by the curtain, he opened the panel and came out through the back, leaving coat, sack, and wrist tape in readiness. As soon as Bessie stepped past the curtain edge into the cabinet, Houdini took her place there, giving her time to get behind the trunk. The handclapping was a neat touch; Houdini himself made the claps, about a second apart, though the audience supposed that Bessie provided the sounds. When Harry opened the curtain a few seconds later, Bess was already in the trunk.

There, she closed the panel, slid into the coat and wrist tapes and pulled the sack up over her. With the slack rope system, it was necessary to keep the loop drawn downward, so the knotted rope would still be tight at the finish. That, however, was simple, even when the wrists were tied.

Other systems could be used for escaping from the sack and entering it again, but the general procedure was the same. The assistant—in this case Mrs. Houdini—found ample time to get back into the precise position that Houdini had left while he was superintending the removal of the ropes and the unlocking of the trunk.

In one of the earlier forms of the Box Trick, a sliding board was used instead of a secret panel, as in the Substitution Trunk. Houdini had improved the trick from its older style by the time he played the Alhambra Theatre; and he had a new trunk specially made for Hardeen to use in Germany, when he went there to fill engagements that Houdini was unable to play because of previous commitments.

Houdini's Handcuff Act

IT WAS AS the "King of Handcuffs" that Houdini first bounded into fame and during the early years of the twentieth century he sometimes styled himself Harry "Handcuff" Houdini, as a token of his achievement. For what Houdini did, was to take a rather ordinary type of act and turn it into an international sensation by emphasizing the "challenge" feature that not only baffled the public but police as well.

Escapes from chains and other devices had been featured by magicians a hundred years before Houdini's day; and during the intervening century, prestidigitators had slipped from manacles on special occasions, sometimes under difficult conditions. But the Handcuff Act had not come into vogue, partly because the modern type of handcuff had not yet been invented.

While the ratchet handcuff was patented as early as 1862, it was not until the 1870s that some of the better cuffs were devised and still more formidable types appeared in the 1880s. It was in the decade following that magicians began to specialize in handcuff escapes and one of the earliest references to "The Handcuff Act" is found in a book entitled

New Ideas in Magic, by W.H.J. Shaw, which was published in 1902. It states:

> This act was first introduced by Joe Godfrey, followed by Louis Paul, and in the last ten years, several performers have introduced the act to good success ...
>
> The main secret in the act is in having a set of different handcuff keys. The principal keys are Bean Giant, Bean No. 2, Sing Sing, Byrns, Scotland Yards, Trenton Nos. 1 and 2, Harper, Tower, Little Detective, etc. ...
>
> While you can do most of the work with eight or ten keys, it is well to have the full set of forty-five keys. When you get into a town or city, you find out what cuffs the police are using, also find out quietly if there are any special makes of cuffs in the city.
>
> Find out all you can, and have these keys concealed on your person where you can get your hands to them quickly. The opening of handcuffs, if you are prepared for same, is as easy as putting coal into a stove.

Among the "several performers" who had "introduced the act to good success," was Houdini; and Shaw must have known it, for he advertised his book in the magician's magazine, *Mahatma,* which had been running full-page accounts of Houdini's tremendous success as a "top liner" on the Keith Circuit and for a full year in England and on the Continent, before Shaw's book appeared.

But Shaw's explanation of the Handcuff Act was so painfully inadequate that he could not afford to mention Houdini, or the contrast would have been laughable and at Shaw's expense.

Houdini at that time was escaping from any and all handcuffs and shackles after being "thoroughly searched from head to foot, proving that he carries no keys, springs, wires or concealed accessories." He was also "allowing the police to iron him in every conceivable position and with as many cuffs as they wish, the more the merrier."

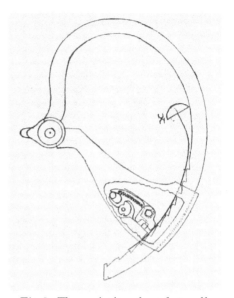

Fig 3. *The majority of ratchet cuffs can be opened by a small piece of fine steel. This is inserted through the handcuff where the lock snaps, X showing the position of the apparatus when inserted in the cuff.*

In England people were paying ten shillings (then $2.40) for standing room to see Houdini's Handcuff Act, which he was performing for as high as $1000 weekly. Shaw, meanwhile, was selling his book at seventy-five cents and offering to furnish all forty-five keys, with "full particulars and pointers" for the sum of $15. So he must have meant the act that Godfrey and Paul once did; not the show that Houdini was putting on right then.

For a real appraisal of Houdini's great Handcuff Act as he presented it during his sensational success in

Fig. 4. *Houdini in full dress, cuffed and shackled, 1903.*

England, we have an excellent review by Ellis Stanyon, who witnessed it during Houdini's two-month return engagement at the Alhambra Theatre in London, beginning December 10, 1900. Referring to Houdini's billing as "The King of Handcuffs," Stanyon stated:

The Handcuff Trick, where a known pattern "cuff" and duplicate keys are used, has for many years been a favorite with so called spirit mediums and magicians who would duplicate their performances, but under a different role.

Mr. Harry Houdini ... has eclipsed anything yet produced in this line, either by mediums or magicians; had the mediums known his secret before he produced his act under the role of a magician, they would doubtless have had another "flutter." Houdini undertakes to free himself from any regulation "iron" or from several at one and the same time, and he invariably succeeds in doing so in less time than it takes to bind him.

I have seen Mr. Houdini with three pairs of strange irons on his wrists, connected with others, equally strange, on his feet; and on another occasion when two sailors from *H.M.S. Powerful,* who evidently took a keen interest in their task, screwed their ship irons on his wrists at the same time trussing him with a broom handle in such a position that he could not even roll into his cabinet, but had to be carried there by the sailors who dropped him in a heap on the floor.

In each of these cases, Houdini succeeded in liberating himself in less time than it took to "fix" him.

He has lately added much to the effect of his act by introducing a small curtained enclosure only just large enough to conceal himself in a crouching position, thus showing that a cabinet is of no consideration beyond a cover to conceal his methods; this is demonstrated by the fact that he will at any time consent to be handcuffed (hands behind) then to kneel inside the tiny enclosure, with front open and while in full view will release himself in a few seconds.

Fig. 5. *Houdini handcuffed and shackled to a ladder.*

The handcuffs are always properly opened and not in any way injured. To ensure the necessary irons being forth-coming, and to maintain interest generally, Houdini offers £100 to any person who shall succeed in "fixing" him—at present the money has not been claimed. He also puts forward a $5,000 challenge to the world, and will forfeit the same to any person who shall duplicate his release from Cuffs, Irons and Strait Jackets under test conditions. That is to strip stark naked, be thoroughly searched, mouth sewed and sealed up, making it impossible to conceal keys, springs or lock pickers; and in that state escape from all fetters that may be locked or laced on arms, legs or body. His ability to accomplish this is endorsed by the Chiefs of Police in the U.S.A., Germany, and by Inspector Melville of Scotland Yard, before all of whom he has submitted to the above test.

An interesting sidelight to Stanyon's account of Houdini's performance was an item which he—Stanyon—published in his magazine, *Magic,* one month later:

> An imitator of Mr. Houdini in his wonderful Handcuff Act and Trunk Trick appeared on January 14th, at the Tivoli, Leeds, in the person of Mr. Theo Hardeen, who announces that he uses no prepared or trick cuffs and further that he will forfeit £20 to anyone who can open and escape from the manacles used in his act and from which he releases himself. Mr. Hardeen, who hails from the States, caused quite a sensation, and has undoubtedly established a reputation.

Apparently, Stanyon, though well informed magically, had not yet learned that Houdini and Hardeen were brothers; that Hardeen at that time worked a second show, a replica of Houdini's own, so that Hardeen could still play a territory after Houdini left to fill engagements elsewhere.

Though Hardeen continued to do the Handcuff Act after Houdini switched to other escapes, the mere fact that it could be duplicated showed that it depended on secret methods and mechanical knowledge, as much as special skill. Showmanship figured strongly, too, but the fact stood that Houdini's work was neither unique nor superhuman, where the regular handcuff routine was concerned.

But it went a long way beyond the mere possession of $15 worth of standard keys. Even with those available, many handcuff workers would have been "sunk"

Fig. 6. *Houdini studying cuff.*

when confronted by situations which Houdini accepted as commonplace. Meeting a real challenge was something more strenuous and exacting than going through a set routine on the performer's own terms. Keys and how to use them were the prime adjunct to the Handcuff Act for one definite reason: handcuffs, unlike padlocks and many other types of locks, did not require their own keys for each individual set. All cuffs of one pattern or model, could be opened with a single master key that was provided with all of that particular make.

In his "challenge" Houdini specified that he would escape from any "regulation hand cuffs" that were in "proper working order," which definitely eliminated a lot of troublesome cuffs; but he still had to be ready for rare or unusual types, the sort that a small-time escape artist would seldom encounter. What was more, Houdini could not back down when properly challenged, considering the bold degree to which he staked his reputation.

Houdini had keys to every known type of cuff, but he also devised special keys that would unlock those of several patterns. Oddly, Houdini struck luck in England, where challenges came thick and heavy; for in his *Conjurers' Magazine,* Houdini wrote:

> It may come as a surprise to many to know that in the British Isles the variety of make of handcuffs is very limited—seven or eight at the utmost.

> In America however, the number reaches about 175 (or more), while on the Continent padlocks are added to the ordinary list of manacles. So one would need be an expert of "picklocks" to get along outside the United Kingdom.

There was also the chance of being confronted with American cuffs in England or elsewhere, so Houdini's early experience with many types of cuffs gave him a decided edge over most of the competitors who cropped up in England. Houdini's "split key," which could be spread to larger size to engage the interior thread in a handcuff lock, was suitable to almost all English cuffs. Thus, with that lone key, he was sometimes equipped to meet a full challenge.

But knowledge of how to use the keys was sometimes more important than the keys themselves. The "Bean Giant" is a striking example of this. Unlike most handcuffs, which are connected by steel links, the Bean Giant has a solid block of metal between the cuffs, so hampering the hands that it is impossible to reach the lock with the key if the keyhole faces away from the fingers.

Nor can the keyhole be reached if the key is held between the teeth and the handcuff brought to it. So to "beat" the Bean Giant, Houdini utilized an extension rod with a key on the end of it. The end of the rod was held between the teeth and the key used to unlock the cuffs.

One way of unlocking certain cuffs is to have a slot cut in the piping of the cabinet, so that a key can be wedged there and the cuffs brought to it. Unlocking cuffs behind the back requires special ability and considerable practice. Houdini's overall secret was a combination of expert technique, skill, patience, strength, and the acquisition of the necessary keys and fakes to suit the individual occasion.

Concealment of the keys was quite simple when presenting the regular stage act. Even Houdini did not undergo an exhaustive search when doing his usual vaudeville turn, as time would not allow it. The fact that he was willing to submit to any challenge or test when occasion called was convincing enough to the average audience.

So Houdini was able to stow the necessary keys in secret pockets, or even in a special key bag, strapped to the leg beneath the knee. Such methods were used by other escape artists, so they were known to Houdini; but it is a question how often he may have used them, because he had something much better.

After Houdini's death, it was revealed on good authority that he had invented and used a secret belt that was made of thin, flexible steel, containing special compartments within what amounted to a double wall. Not only that, the inner belt ran on tiny ball bearings so that it could be revolved by mere pressure from Houdini's arm. Wherever his hands were placed, whatever key or pick he may have required, Houdini could gain when he wanted it. This solved the biggest bugaboo in handcuff work; the accessibility of a required tool. Often, an escape artist might be locked so that he could not get at the gadget he needed most, but Houdini's special belt solved that dilemma for him, which is probably why it remained such a closely guarded secret.

Reserve keys were frequently hidden in the piping of the cabinet and one escape artist stowed them in the loose seams of a huge gold initial that was embroidered on the inner wall of his cloth cabinet. Houdini's cabinet was well fitted with hiding places for "gags" and "fakes" and even files for handcuff work; but he had a better system which he described in his notes:

> A small tube or opening, fitted into the side or back of the cabinet; this to allow an assistant to slide in any special key or device which might be required. Such a system would make it unnecessary to stock the cabinet with small appliances; these could be obtained from offstage and slipped in after the inspection.

Fig. 7. *Houdini in multiple handcuffs, 1903.*

This meant that if Houdini happened to be confronted with strange or difficult handcuffs, he could let himself be locked in them and depend on an assistant to provide him with the type of gadget needed to spring the cuff. But there were simpler ways to deal with such shackles.One of Houdini' s systems was to have his wrists locked with four or five pairs of handcuffs. The "strange" pair was placed highest up, where his forearms were so much thicker than his wrists that Houdini could simply slip off those cuffs after unlocking the pairs below.[1]

This method was particularly good when the other cuffs were the sort that could be opened rapidly, that is, standard cuffs to which Houdini had quickly available keys, so he could work in the "open" fashion described in Stanyon's reviews.

Hardeen, who continued to do the Handcuff Act after Houdini had switched to more spectacular escapes, also

---

1 Many people thought that Houdini could slip cuffs that were tightly locked about his wrists, but he found that impossible. He even tried compressing the knuckles of his hands in special clamps for hours at a time, hoping to reduce their girth, but it was of no avail; so he gave it up.

used the same system. With English cuffs, Hardeen often eliminated the cabinet entirely and simply had an assistant throw a large cloth over his handcuffed wrists and arms. He would then work the cuffs free and fling them from beneath the cloth. If a pair of formidable cuffs were placed highest up, they would come off last of all, making the climax all the stronger.

Another way of dealing with difficult cuffs was to use them as connecting links, in a chain of three handcuffs. One wrist would be placed behind the neck, with a hand cuff attached and dangling downward. The "strange" cuffs would be linked to that; then locked to another, which in turn would be locked around the other wrist. All that was necessary was to unlock the "regular" cuffs and the middle pair would fall free.

Similarly, a chain of cuffs could be run from a pair linked to the wrists to a set of leg irons that were around the ankles. Again, the strange cuffs would form the middle unit in a chain of three, so they would drop free when the others were unlocked.

Persons who have never witnessed a Handcuff Act—and very few today have—may logically ask: "But what did people say when the handcuffs were returned still locked?"

They were all the more awed. That was because *all* hand-cuffs were *always* returned locked. When Houdini opened a pair, he immediately locked them again. That was why people thought that he had slipped them, or had removed them by some uncanny power. So the "strange" cuffs, that were never unlocked at all, were accepted in the same astounded way.

Houdini, showman that he was, welcomed all "freak" handcuffs. Usually they were brought on to the stage by someone who had bought them in a secondhand store. Houdini would look at the outmoded relics and demand: "Do you know what these are?" When the owner replied, "No," Houdini would turn to the audience and declare in a tone of denunciation: "These are antique torture cuffs. They have been brought here to trick me. They are not regulation cuffs, so I do not have to accept them. But I will!"

Sometimes the cuffs were easy and Houdini knew it. But often there could be an actual "trick" behind those nonregulation handcuffs. Or sometimes a pair of cuffs with a strictly modern look could rouse his suspicions, too. Always, smart challengers were seeking a way to catch Houdini unaware. He could meet that, too.

His system was this: He would insist on trying the key, to make sure that it worked the lock. In so doing, he would let an assistant get a good look at the key. The assistant would go off stage to a trunk where Houdini carried hundreds of odd keys and would pick up one resembling the key to the freak cuffs. After the spectator had locked Houdini in the freak pair, the assistant would take the real key and give "it" to another committee man to hold.

In so doing, the assistant would "switch" his own odd key for the one that belonged to the freak handcuffs. The assistant would then slip the real key to Houdini when he went into the cabinet. Houdini would free himself from the difficult handcuffs—thanks to the fact that he had the key belonging to them!—and after handing the cuffs to the amazed owner, he would go to the man who held the dummy and switch it back for the real key. He would then return the genuine key to its owner.

That would be hard to go one better, but Houdini often did.

When he had sufficient time, he would make a quick switch himself and send the real key off stage, where it could be duplicated with equipment that Houdini carried with the act. That was done while Houdini was examining other cuffs and accepting or rejecting them as the case might be.

By then, an assistant brought back the original key and slipped it to Houdini. He took the dummy from the man who was holding it and made another switch, so that he gave the real key to its owner. Meanwhile, an assistant was getting ready to slip the duplicate to Houdini when he went into the cabinet. Those handcuffs were as good as off before Houdini even put them on.

In contrast to such difficult situations, there were times when the Handcuff Act was simplicity itself. Far from needing keys to open cuffs, Houdini had other ways. He had found by experiment with British handcuffs that most of the regulation types of that period could be knocked open by a hard blow delivered in the right place.

That was something of a tribute to the quality of the hand-cuff. Anything can be broken if smashed hard enough; and those cuffs were strong enough to take a beating. But in the course of it, the spring would give, causing the handcuff to open without a key.

For that purpose, Houdini used a strip of lead strapped to his leg like a key bag. He hit the cuffs against it and opened them soundlessly as the cloth of the trouser leg reduced the noise of the impact to a dull thud. What was more, he could do it with the locks of the handcuffs sealed. That made it look like something really supernormal.

Houdini also used special picks that could open cuffs without working on the keyhole. One of the simplest but most effective was a strip of steel, three and a half inches long and only one quarter inch wide, which could be wedged under the ratchet of a handcuff. With this, Houdini could spring all cuffs of that type except the formidable double-lock cuffs that had to be opened with keys.

While Houdini avoided use of confederates from the audience, the "planting" of regulation handcuffs was allowable by the terms of his act.

This meant that when Houdini called for a committee to come on stage, he would be sure that handcuffs would be brought up. All members of the committee were allowed to inspect any cuffs that Houdini put on, so "planted" cuffs were legitimate in every way.

Fig. 8. *Russian poster or challenge for Houdini in handcuffs.*

The more standard cuffs, the better, as it gave Houdini choice of those he could shed with the greatest ease. This sped the act and allowed the escape to be done more openly. It also reduced the percentage of troublesome freak cuffs. With plenty of others offered by the committee, Houdini could reject any that might be fixed to hamper his act.

Handcuffs could be fixed the other way about; that was, they could be "faked" to open without key or pick. The best way of "tricking" a regulation handcuff was to replace its strong interior spring with a weak one.

It could then pass ordinary inspection, but any hard knock would open it; or, with a sufficiently weak spring, the cuff could actually be pulled open by an opposite tug of the wrists.

The only times Houdini or Hardeen used such handcuffs was when making a jump from a bridge into a river, so as to effect a "full view" escape before a vast crowd. The "jump cuffs," as the trick types were called, could be switched for a pair of regulation irons that had first been thoroughly examined, one being outwardly the exact duplicate of the other.

The "jump cuffs" were pulled open immediately after hitting the water, enabling Houdini to come to the surface freed and unencumbered. A leap from a bridge while hand-cuffed was classed as a publicity stunt, not a bona fide challenge. Since a pair of special cuffs insured quick results and minimized the danger, they were valid in such cases.

Houdini's Jail Escapes

ALTHOUGH THE HANDCUFF ACT rocketed Houdini to fame, the factor that triggered such success was actually his "Jail Escape" or more correctly, the series of "jail breaks" which he accomplished in order to prove himself the "Elusive American" that he continually claimed to be.

Contrary to a legend that occasionally crops up, Houdini did not overwhelm the British public overnight by escaping from a jail cell at Scotland Yard. He had gained his reputation as a "prison breaker" when playing various towns and cities in the United States. What he actually did was visit the "Yard" and escape from a pair of regulation handcuffs that Superintendent Melville placed on him.

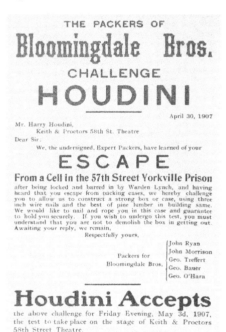

THE PACKERS OF

Bloomingdale Bros.

CHALLENGE

HOUDINI

April 30, 1907

Mr. Harry Houdini,
Keith & Proctors 58th St. Theatre
Dear Sir:
We, the undersigned, Expert Packers, have learned of your

ESCAPE

From a Cell in the 57th Street Yorkville Prison
after being locked and barred in by Warden Lynch, and having heard that you escape from packing cases, we hereby challenge you to allow us to construct a strong box or case, using three inch wire nails and the best of pine lumber in building same. We would like to nail and rope you in this case and guarantee to hold you securely. If you wish to undergo this test, you must understand that you are not to demolish the box in getting out. Awaiting your reply, we remain,

Respectfully yours,

Packers for
Bloomingdale Bros,

{ John Ryan
John Morrison
Geo. Treffert
Geo. Bauer
Geo. O'Hara

Houdini Accepts

the above challenge for Friday Evening, May 3d, 1907, the test to take place on the stage of Keith & Proctors 58th Street Theatre.

$500 WILL BE HANDED TO ANYONE FINDING ANY PREPARATION IN THE ABOVE CASE

Fig. 9

37

Moreover, he did it so convincingly and in such swift, surprising fashion, that Melville himself was nonplused. Present at the time was the manager of the Alhambra Theatre, who had promised Houdini an engagement if he could talk Scotland Yard into a "test" of their manacles. As it worked out, Houdini didn't have to go beyond the superintendent's office to prove his claim.

Fig. 10. *Houdini handcuffed to cell door in cell block.*

Later, however, Houdini made many jail escapes in England and on the Continent. He made many more after his return to America and his files contained hundreds of letters from police chiefs attesting that the escapes were bona fide. This should be particularly stressed to appraise Houdini's jail escapes at their true worth, as many imitators made false or exaggerated claims as to their ability in that line, many being totally unsubstantiated.

Here is a verbatim account of one of Houdini's sensational "jail breaks" taken from the *Sheffield Independent* of Wednesday, January 20, 1904, with the police affidavit appended:

> Harry Houdini, the World-Famous Prison Breaker and Handcuff Expert, who is this week performing at the Empire Palace of Varieties, was yesterday given an opportunity of showing his skill in the police cells at Water Lane.
>
> He presented himself to the chief constable with the idea of arranging a private display during the week, but Commander Scott unexpectedly asked him to try what he could do at once. He was marched off to the cells on the upper corridor and was stripped of the whole of his clothes, which were placed in an adjoining cell, the door of which was then triple locked with a master key.
>
> The apartment in which he was to be locked—the redoubtable one, by the way, in which Charles Peace was placed after his apprehension—was then thoroughly searched and the door was triple locked upon Houdini.
>
> At the artiste's request the whole of the cells on the corridor were also locked and the iron gate at the foot of the steps, which is secured with a seven-lever lock, was secured.

Houdini, previous to being incarcerated, asked if he was not out in twenty minutes the door should be opened for him, but to the surprise of the chief constable and the few other people present, the jail breaker joined the party on the bottom corridor exactly five minutes after he had been left.

In this marvelously short space of time he got out of the cell, opened the apartment where his clothes were secured, dressed himself with the exception of his collar and his tie, unfastened the remaining cells in the row, and burst open the iron gate. Before he left the prison, Houdini was presented with the following certificate:

CHIEF CONSTABLE'S OFFICE

Sheffield, Jan. 19, 1904

This is to certify that Mr. Harry Houdini was this day stripped stark naked and locked in the cell which once contained Charles Peace. The cell was searched and triple-locked, but Mr. Houdini released himself and redressed in five minutes, having also opened the iron gate of the corridor.

Charles J. Scott, Commander (R.N.)
Chief Constable, Sheffield.
Witness to the foregoing feat,
George H. Barker, Deputy Chief Constable.

The reference to Charles Peace was particularly appropriate because Peace, one of the most notorious burglars and murderers in the annals of English crime, had also shown a penchant for escapes, his most famous being a leap from the window of a railway carriage traveling at express speed, while he was being taken to his trial. But even Peace had regarded an attempted escape as hopeless from the very cell that Houdini was to crack with ease, a few decades later!

In Liverpool, Houdini staged another spectacular jail escape, which was described in the *London Daily Express* of February 3, 1904. The article carried this statement:

To Whom It May Concern:

I certify that today, Mr. Harry Houdini showed his abilities in releasing himself from restraint.

He had three pairs of handcuffs, one a very close-fitting pair, placed round his wrists and he was placed in a nude state in a cell which had previously been searched.

Within six minutes, he was free from the handcuffs, had opened the cell door, and had opened the doors of all the other cells in the corridor, had changed a prisoner from one cell to another and had so securely locked him in that he had to be asked to unlock the door.

> (Signed) Leonard Dunning,
> Head Constable, Liverpool.

Feb. 2, 1904.

In Washington, D.C., on January 6, 1906, Houdini escaped from Cell Number 2 of Murderers' Row in the U.S. Jail, the cell in which Charles Guiteau, the assassin of President Garfield, had been imprisoned for nearly a year. He then proceeded to open the doors of eight other cells and shuffle their occupants about, so that each was found in a different cell when Houdini called officials to the scene, about twenty minutes later.

Houdini obtained certificates both from Warden J. H. Harris and Superintendent Richard Sylvester, covering that occasion, on which he was stripped and searched as usual. In his affidavit, Superintendent Sylvester stated:

> The experiment was a very valuable one in that the department has been instructed as to the adoption of further security which will protect any lock from being opened or interfered with. The act was interesting and profitable, and worthy of study.

Most spectacular of all, however, was Houdini's escape from the Boston City Prison on March 19, 1906, where Superintendent of Police, William H. Pierce personally clamped Houdini in handcuffs and leg irons; then locked him in a cell on the second tier.

In about twenty minutes, Houdini not only escaped from the manacles and cell; he went through the other cells, looking for a prisoner to lock in the one he had left; regained his clothes from a locked cell on the lower tier; scaled the prison wall and reached the theater, half a mile away, where he phoned Superintendent Pierce to tell him all that had happened.

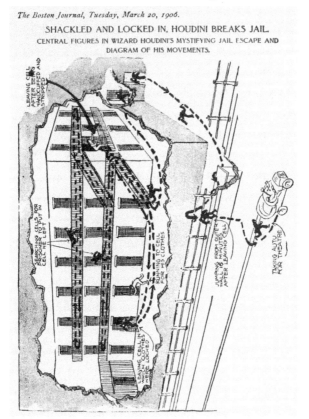

The Boston Journal, Tuesday, March 20, 1906.

SHACKLED AND LOCKED IN, HOUDINI BREAKS JAIL.
CENTRAL FIGURES IN WIZARD HOUDINI'S MYSTIFYING JAIL ESCAPE AND
DIAGRAM OF HIS MOVEMENTS.

Fig. 11. *Diagram of Houdini's jail escape, 1906.*

Dozens of other instances could be cited and described in detail, but suffice it that Houdini was always ready to attempt a jail escape under the most exacting conditions. It was prior to such escapes that he was most thoroughly searched for implements; and generally, the searchers were looking for handcuff keys as well, for Houdini allowed himself to be shackled in the cell, as already described.

Whenever possible, Houdini first paid a visit to the jail cell and tested the lock with its key. That was fair enough, just as with handcuffs. He had a right to see whether or not the lock was in working order; and if he had backed down, it would have been tantamount to failure.

Once Houdini had brief possession of the key, he could sometimes make a wax impression of it. This could be done by having a small box open at one end, with a bed of soft wax inside. A box used to hold safety razor blades was about the proper size. The impression was gained by placing the end of the key into the box and pressing it down into the wax. From that, a duplicate could be made later.

Getting such impressions could be very easy. Sometimes the turnkey was simply told to let Houdini have a look at the key. Often, the light was bad in the corridor, so Houdini had to carry the key to a spot where he could study it more closely. This gave him a chance to make the impression before returning it, the turnkey suspecting nothing.

Sometimes Houdini was handed a master key that fitted all the cells in the block. When it had been duplicated from the wax impression, Houdini had a potent implement indeed. It enabled him to unlock cells in rapid-fire style, once witnesses had retired from the scene. Other prisoners didn't know what was happening, so fast did Houdini work.

A good look at the key or lock was sometimes all that Houdini needed to provide himself with a suitable key or pick.

In difficult cases, a second visit to the jail was helpful, as it offered a chance to try the special key when looking over the lock again.

Quite often Houdini relied on an associate to obtain a key beforehand, either by the wax impression or through a study of the lock. Unquestionably there were times when information regarding certain jail locks could be gained through records or from local locksmiths. This enabled Houdini to pay his first visit already equipped for an escape.

A lock of a spring latch type could be temporarily fixed by jamming a wooden wedge into the socket. Houdini never overlooked that opportunity. The wedge was pushed in place just before the door was clanged shut and the lock would either fail to catch or would catch so slightly that a hard jolt would knock it loose. After his escape, Houdini would remove the wedge.

On one occasion, Houdini went to look over a jail cell accompanied by his brother Hardeen. The lock was formidable, but of the spring latch type. While the police chief was asking Houdini why he didn't try to make the escape then and there, Houdini suddenly decided that he would.

Houdini whispered a quick word to Hardeen and while Houdini was being searched, Hardeen pulled a sheet of paper from a notebook, wadded it tightly, and edged close enough to the door to jam the wad into the latch socket. Houdini was put into the cell naked, keyless, and presumably defeated; but the police chief and the jailer had scarcely turned away before they heard the door clang again behind them and there was Houdini free!

He had opened the door, pulled out the paper wad, and flipped it through the barred window of the cell as he slammed the door behind him, all in a matter of seconds.

Some escapes, of course, took longer. Always, there was the job of hiding the key or pick, when one was needed, as it generally was. One of Houdini's systems was to hide the key in his shaggy hair.

He would have a dab of adhesive wax on the key, which was secretly palmed in one of his hands; and he would insist that his hair be examined first. That done, he would run his hand through his hair, leaving the key there, the wax holding it in place.

Another method was to fix the key under his instep with a strip of adhesive tape. Often, it was possible for Houdini to lay the key in some unnoticed spot on the floor; just past a chair leg for example, and after his feet had been examined, he had only to step on the hidden key and his foot would pick up the tape.

A clever system was to wear a pair of slippers into the cell, to avoid foot contact with the cold floor. The slippers were checked to see that no keys had been dropped into them. Each slipper had a hollow heel that swiveled open by pressing a hidden catch. The needed keys were in the hollow heels.

Sometimes a key was gummed beneath a bench on which Houdini was seated when handcuffed in the cell. A still neater trick was this: Just before being examined, Houdini would take a last look at the lock to make sure he was willing to go through with the escape. He had a gummed key palmed and simply stuck it beneath the bulky lock itself. When locked in the cell, he had only to reclaim the key from that hiding place.

The hooked key was another handy gadget. Just a key or a pick with a hook soldered to it. Just before being examined, Houdini would brush the back of a man's shoulder and hook the key there. After the examination, he would reverse the process and regain the key. Usually, he had a friend on hand to "assist" in this, as a stranger might have turned around too soon. All the friend had to do was keep his back away from view. Houdini did the rest.

After a really grueling search, Houdini always had a last resort. Once he thrust his hands through the bars of the jail cell and shook hands with the committee to show that he was willing to accept defeat in a sporting fashion. The last man to shake Houdini's hand was his one friend on the committee.

The friend was wearing a finger ring with a spring clip soldered to it, holding the key hidden in his palm. During the fervent handshake, Houdini drew the hidden key from the clip and all was set.

Another story goes that just prior to a jail escape, Houdini's wife rushed to the cell and impetuously gave him a long farewell kiss through the bars. Neither spoke a word during that impassioned parting. They couldn't. The key was in Mrs. Houdini's mouth at the start, and it wound up in Houdini's at the finish.

In doing handcuff escapes under rigid search conditions, Houdini had to use these same ingenious ways of obtaining keys, exactly as with the jail cell escape. If confronted by a real tough task, Houdini often would appear briefly from the cabinet—still handcuffed—to assure the audience that he intended to keep on with the escape.

Since the work was strenuous, he would sometimes ask for a drink of water. That was brought to him in a cup. In the cup was a needed key or an extra pick, which he secretly obtained in his month while drinking the water.

It should be remembered that Houdini's facility with the Needle Trick enabled him to show his mouth empty despite a thorough examination; so, it was quite feasible for him to conceal small keys in the same fashion. However, he allowed his mouth to be sealed, when demanded; so that would not always work. One thing was certain: Houdini's ingenuity always saw him through; one way or another.

Imitators used all sort of means to match Houdini's bona fide jail escapes; anything from bribing petty officials at small jails to outright misrepresentation of the facts. Anyone could escape from a cell if a key was slipped to him. If such a "fix" could not be arranged, an escape artist would simply go to the jail and offer to show how he could get out of regulation handcuffs.

His manager would then suggest that the escape artist use a cell as a cabinet, while working on the cuffs. The cell, however, would not be locked.

But the account given to the local newspaper or "planted". through an obliging reporter, would state that the Great So-and-So escaped from regulation irons and emerged from the cell where he had been placed by the police. Many such claims found their way into print during the heyday of the Handcuff Act, but they all had the false ring of theatrical press notices, with the exception of the descriptions of Houdini's exploits, which made authentic headlines.

Houdini's Card Scaling

IN HIS EARLY CAREER Houdini advertised himself as the "King of Cards," and he was without doubt one of the master manipulators of his time. Being a showman, he aimed for the spectacular in his card work, so while he was well versed in more subtle sleights, he stressed card flourishes in his public performances.

One of his favorite feats at magicians' gatherings was that of scaling cards, boomerang fashion, and catching them in a deft manner. When he put on his full evening show, Houdini made this a feature and won great acclaim for his skill. Two of his best stunts were those of catching a scaled card in the pack itself; and cutting a card in midair with a pair of scissors.

Both depend on the "boomerang" toss, which is done as follows:

First, hold a playing card between the first two fingers of the right hand, which grip it edgeways and turn the card inward, at right angles to the palm. Now, if the hand is snapped forward, with an action of the wrist, the card, when simultaneously released, will scale some distance through the air.

By bringing the hand back to the shoulder, a throwing action is added, so that once the full knack is acquired, cards can be skimmed clear to the balcony of a theater. Houdini was adept at this and, like many other performers, had his own favorite grip. Some, for example, prefer to hold the card between the middle fingers, which may be better for the distance " throw" but not for the "boomerang" about to be described.

The reason is this:

The boomerang is a double action, a short scaling throw combined with a rapid spin that brings it back to the hand, although it may travel a considerable distance during flight, making it all the more effective.

To add the needed spin, the tip of the forefinger is moved to the outer right corner of the card, pressing lightly against the corner. The thumb moves over and replaces the forefinger, pressing the card lightly down against the second finger which is still beneath.

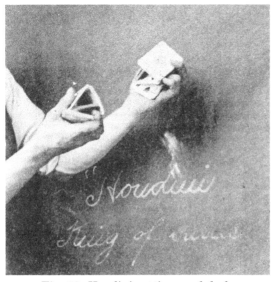

Now the card is given an easy scale, at an upward angle without too hard an outward snap of the wrist. This is a modified throw which might scale the card some twenty or thirty feet, if gripped *between* the fingers; in fact, it is good to experiment that way

Fig. 12. *Houdini cutting card deck.*

first and note how the card tends to "hook back" near the finish of the flight.

But with the boomerang, the forefinger is used to speed the spin. In completing its forward, upward toss, the wrist provides a sharp, downward, inward jerk, so that the forefinger catches the corner of the card as it starts on its way, turning it into a veritable whirligig.

While the card is still scaling upward and outward, the faster spin takes over and brings it back almost along its original path. With practice, the forward and backward actions can be so nicely equalized that the card will come almost to the hand. Short tosses should be tried at first, the simplest being to send the card almost straight upward, when both the scale and the spin can be handled rather lazily, since the card tends to come down to where it started from.

From that, the tyro can work gradually to a forty-five degree angle, which is both showy and effective. More distance can be gained through practice, but too much is not necessary, as the card's comparatively slow progress through the air makes it appear to go farther than it actually does.

The simplest way to recapture the returning card is to swoop the hand down on it, catching the card flat. But Houdini made it all the more effective in the ways already mentioned. First:

In the Pack

The pack is held crosswise in the left hand, thumb along the left side, fingers at the right. The right hand tosses the single card, boomerang fashion; then goes directly to the pack, gripping it endwise, fingers at the outer end, thumb at the inner.

This enables the hands to open the pack book-fashion, at the same time thrusting the gap toward the returning card. The pack should be opened at the left side, with a slight lift of the outer end as well, thus presenting the outer left corner to the card as it arrives, giving it that much more space in which to land.

In case the card's flight is slightly misgauged, the halves of the pack can be completely separated and then quickly brought together, trapping the card between them.

The one-hand version of the "pack catch" is much neater and correspondingly more difficult. That was the way in which Houdini worked it. Basically, the system is the same, except that the left hand alone holds the pack and the left side is lifted with the thumb, to provide the gap.

This is very similar to the "lift" or separation made with a sleight known to magicians as the "Charlier Pass," but the left thumb should be kept close to the inner corner of the pack, so as to allow more room for the arriving card at the outer left corner. In this case, the halves of the pack cannot be taken clear apart, so naturally more skill is needed, as well as better judgment of the flying card's course.

Cutting Card with Scissors

Houdini made a great "show" of this trick, which requires long practice in order to toss the card and then cut it by taking the scissors in the same hand. The difficulty is clue to the time required to obtain the scissors after the card is tossed.

Assuming that the right hand scales the card, the scissors can be laid loose and slightly open in the left; but it still requires a fairly long throw to give the right hand time to grab the scissors "blind" and have them ready for the spinning card's arrival.

The larger the scissors the better, as they are easier to grab and provide a larger gap to receive the card, along with more cutting surface. The blades are opened, thrust directly at the spinning card and clipped fast together, the moment it clicks between them.

Large scissors add to the effect, as they show up better and look more difficult to handle, although the opposite is the case. By tossing the cards with the right hand and having the scissors ready in the left, the time interval is no longer a problem, but the cut is not so effective as the single-handed version.

The Straitjacket Escape

THE ESCAPE from a straitjacket was made famous both by Houdini and his brother Hardeen, though it is likely neither had even heard of a straitjacket, let alone tried to get out of one, at the time when they appeared together as the Houdini Brothers, in 1893.

Houdini stated that when he played Saint John, New Brunswick, a few years later, he saw and tried out a straitjacket of the type used to confine the murderous insane. Always observant, Houdini noted that by putting strain on the shoulder, it would be possible to gain enough slack to free the arms.

He practiced this, even to the extent of dislocating his shoulder to effect the escape, but it was not until 1900, when he had gained fame as a "Handcuff King" and was taking on challenges from the police, that he turned the straitjacket release into a real sensation.

Without the challenge, audiences were lukewarm to this type of escape, when effected out of sight, in the confines of a curtained cabinet. They took it that the escapist simply wriggled out without too much difficulty, which was actually the case when amateurs performed it, using what were virtually "trick" straitjackets.

But in 1900, at the Wintergarten in Berlin, and in 1901 in Hanover, Houdini met police challenges with their own straitjackets, the latter escape taking him an hour and a half of what he described as "pain, torture, agony and misery."

A typical regulation straitjacket is made of heavy canvas, reinforced with leather, which forms the collar and cuffs, as well as the various straps. The cuffs have no outlets for the hands; instead, they are like elongated bags, terminating in leather straps that go around the body and are buckled in back.

The collar and jacket open at the back, and are provided with straps, so that after the prisoner's arms have been thrust into the sleeves, the jacket itself can be strapped about him, the sleeves being strapped last. The straps are sewn or riveted to the straitjacket.

In addition to the neck, chest, hip, and sleeve straps, other straps may be provided, making the jacket all the more formidable, its whole purpose being to restrain the strongest and most violent insane or prisoners, many of whom become utterly exhausted in a futile struggle against its toils.

During Houdini's appearance in Germany, in 1900, he was unable to fulfill continued engagements because of scheduled appearances in England. So rapid arrangements were made to bring his brother Theo to Germany, where he opened at the Olympia Theatre in Magdeburg, in July 1900. While his act was an exact duplicate of Houdini's, he had to appear under another name to avoid misrepresentation. So the name "Hardeen" was established.

The billing read in part:

> Hardeen is the only artist who works in exactly the same manner as Houdini and as a result of his success in London has been rightfully called Houdini the Second. Therefore, if the Directors of the Alhambra cannot release Houdini from his engagement, Hardeen will appear here both for afternoon and evening performances, just as if Houdini would be here in person.

From then on, Hardeen continued to appear with an act similar to Houdini's and with it accepted many challenges. As the straitjacket was one, Hardeen practiced the escape and later, like Houdini, made a feature of it. So the escape, as here described, is a composite of the two and incorporates advice from both masters of the art of shedding a troublesome straitjacket.

From the moment that either Houdini or Hardeen went into the straitjacket, the immediate job was to obtain slack.

As the hands were thrust into the sleeves,

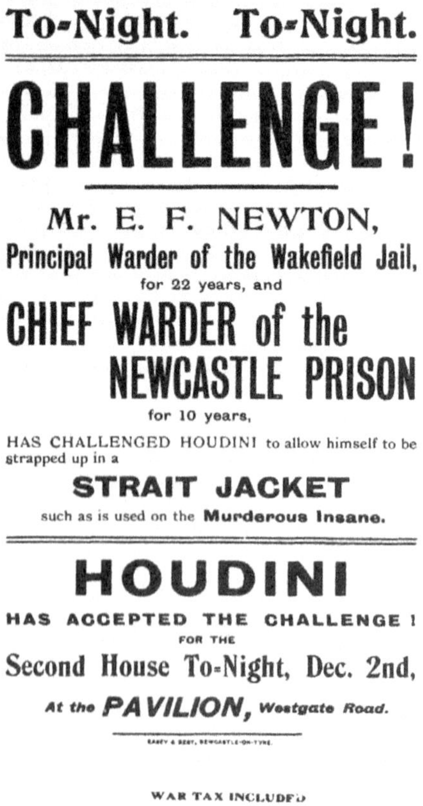

To-Night. To-Night.

CHALLENGE!

Mr. E. F. NEWTON,
Principal Warder of the Wakefield Jail,
for 22 years, and

CHIEF WARDER of the NEWCASTLE PRISON
for 10 years,

HAS CHALLENGED HOUDINI to allow himself to be strapped up in a

STRAIT JACKET
such as is used on the **Murderous Insane.**

HOUDINI
HAS ACCEPTED THE CHALLENGE !
FOR THE
Second House To-Night, Dec. 2nd,
At the *PAVILION,* Westgate Road.

WAR TAX INCLUDED

Fig. 13

the fingers gripped as much loose cloth as possible, to keep from going the full depth. Naturally, this could not be over-done, or it would excite suspicion. But it gave the escape artist a start—even though sometimes trifling—that an ordinary prisoner might totally miss.

Chest expansion was even more important, as in all escapes where the performer is tightly bound about the body. Houdini had a tremendous chest expansion, which he cultivated for underwater escapes and Hardeen developed one almost as great. This enabled them to strain against the body straps; but it was also effective to let the body be pulled along when the straps were being tightened, the purpose in both actions being to preserve slack.

Most important was the placement of the arms when the committee came to them. They were crossed, not folded; that is, one arm was simply placed over the other, instead of interlocking them. While the sleeve straps were being tightened, the hands kept their grip on the cloth inside the sleeves and the chest was again expanded, to gain all possible slack.

Houdini explained that in the actual escape, the first job was to work the arms up over the head, the upper overlying arm first. This could be helped by pressing the elbow on something solid, thus forcing the arm upward through sheer strength. Once sufficiently free, the arms were brought in front of the body, so that the buckles of the sleeve straps could be undone with the teeth.

Then the hands, working through the canvas, go after the neck buckles and the body buckles, which, by dint of long practice, can be loosened despite that handicap. Getting the jacket off the arms and body is the final task. This is done by stepping on the ends of the sleeves and giving an upward, backward pull. Another way is to fasten the sleeve buckle all over again, insert one foot in the loop as in a stirrup, and pull away the jacket while lying on the back.

There are many varieties of straitjackets, some being made entirely of leather.

Those collected by Houdini and Hardeen present a formidable array, some really looking like the "torture devices" which they could literally prove to be, when used to put the "squeeze" on a victim.

Fig. 14. *An all-leather torture strait-jacket which Houdini featured in Scotland. There were straps tied from the tips of the gauntlets to the ankles. Sidney Radner, Holyoke, Massachusetts, escapologist, is wearing the jacket.*

In more difficult challenges, particularly when the arms were actually folded, it was necessary to dislocate the shoulder of the top arm in order to get free. Houdini could dislocate either shoulder, so he could let the committee strap him up the way they wanted. Hardeen could only throw his right arm out of joint, so he always worked with his right arm on top. Naturally, the simpler the jacket or the more loosely it was strapped, the easier and quicker the escape became.

But under true challenge conditions, it usually proved quite strenuous. However, since the escape was made inside a curtained cabinet—as was usual with most escapes—the audience did not witness the performer's effort, so the straitjacket release was much work for little credit, particularly as imitators kept cropping up who used "trick" straitjackets that could be peeled off about as easily as a sweater.

Photos of the period showed dozens of would-be "escape kings" shackled in their own handcuffs and their own straitjackets, all of a very "fakey" type. All this detracted from the original act as presented by Houdini and later by Hardeen.

Four years after Houdini's straitjacket escape at the Wintergarten in Berlin, Hardeen took on a similar challenge in London. He effected the escape, but not without great difficulty, and a reaction that he had not anticipated. The event caused enough furor to warrant the following newspaper story:

Hardeen, the "Handcuff King" emerged in a state of evident distress from a cabinet in the Empire Theatre on Wednesday evening and a large assembly looked on amazed. He had accepted a challenge from two police constables who undertook to secure him in a straitjacket and now after a struggle extending over a quarter of an hour, he was free!

To the onlooker, Hardeen's plight was absolutely hopeless, and while he was hidden from view, two policemen kept the cabinet under close observation

... One tried to peep inside and when he was forced back, the audience did not seem at all pleased.

As time went on, people grew indignant and there was some hooting. When at length Hardeen walked, or rather staggered out, his exit was viewed with mixed feelings.

One policeman stepped to the front of the stage and remarked that they were not at all satisfied, because they were convinced that nobody could escape from the jacket unassisted. He invited Hardeen to submit himself to being secured in the jacket again, but naturally the artiste was not at all anxious to do the trick twice the same evening.

Instead, Hardeen agreed to satisfy the skeptics by repeating the escape two nights later, in full view, to prove there was no confederacy. Far from detracting from the Straitjacket Escape, that made it a new sensation and actually more baffling than ever. Here is an excerpt from a news report of that event:

> When Hardeen, the Handcuff King, liberated himself from a straitjacket of the type used to secure the murderous insane, at the Empire a few evenings back, the bulk of those who saw him emerge free from the cabinet refused to believe that he had extricated himself without assistance. There was talk of trap doors and other contrivances, and Hardeen, instead of gaining applause, had to put up with something in the nature of a little demonstration.

But his chance to retaliate came with a vengeance on Friday evening, for as the result of a second challenge, he undertook to get out of the same straitjacket in full view of the audience. Having been securely strapped into the straitjacket, the famous performer remarked good-humoredly that he would expect an apology from those gentlemen when he had freed himself; and an admiring assembly cheered lustily.

To attempt to faithfully describe how Hardeen removed the jacket would be next to impossible, for surprising as it may appear, he undid the bulk of the straps with such rapid movements that nobody seemed able to follow him. Rolling on the stage and turning somersaults, Hardeen appeared to contract certain muscles and having freed one of his arms by a dislocation which would have shattered the bones in the limbs of any ordinary individual, his task was simplified.

The buckles at the back of the jacket were undone last of all, and Hardeen, with hair and clothing disarranged, stepped to the front of the stage to receive an ovation, the like of which has seldom if ever been given at the Empire.

Soon Houdini was working the straitjacket on the open stage and Hardeen made it a regular feature of his act, during his tour of the British music halls.

The straitjacket proved to be excellent as an outdoor attraction as well as a stage show and in later years Houdini performed it before vast crowds while hanging suspended by his feet from a high building. Here is an account that appeared in the *Pittsburgh Sun,* Monday, November 6, 1916:

> A suppressed shout came from the crowd as Houdini appeared in the doorway of the Sun Building. Above him, like a gallows, a single beam projected from a window at the top story of the building and a rope swung clear, coiling in sinister fashion at his *feet* ...
>
> The two attendants pressed close. His arms were inserted in the long, closed sleeves of the strait-jacket. One of the attendants clasped him about the body.... The other, standing behind him, fastened strap after strap ... "Make it tight," came the quiet word from the prisoner.
>
> The man's knee went up for purchase in the small of Houdini's back. Using every ounce of strength, the attendant drew the big strap through the buckle until it would not yield even a sixteenth of an inch more. He caught it there and made it fast.
>
> Then the arms of the prisoner were crossed over his body and the ends of those closed sleeves were brought around in back. Again, the knee was brought into use. Again the strap was pulled to its highest tension. The crowd watched, stirred with a constant murmur and movement.
>
> Then Houdini's ankles were fastened to the rope by a special appliance that prevented injury, but insured

safety. A word was spoken. The two attendants seized the bound man's body. Workmen drew the rope steadily through the pulleys. Houdini's feet went up and as his body cleared the platform, it was released.

The Handcuff King dangled head downward. Each moment he was drawn higher, swaying slightly, spinning dizzily. Up, up, past the windows in the fifth story of the Sun Building, Houdini was drawn.

Then he hung still.

Only for a second. While watches gleamed in the crowd below, the Handcuff King was seen to struggle, not frantically, but with a steady, systematic swelling and contracting of muscles; and almost imperceptible lithe wrigglings of the torso.

The struggle went on. One minute... two... then three. Would Houdini do it? Hundreds in the crowd undoubtedly were asking that question. From above came an inarticulate shout. The muffled arms writhed one after the other over Houdini's head. His hand still encased in the sleeves of the straitjacket, fumbled quickly and effectively with the buckles at his back. Another contortion and the straitjacket slipped down over his chest, over his head, and was flung from his arms to the street in a crumpled heap.

Houdini was free.

The arms waved. Houdini had triumphed—as he always triumphs. Less than a minute later, while the crowd's cheers still rang against the gray walls of surrounding buildings, he slipped down the face of the building to the platform. The attendants received him in a twinkling and he stood erect, unconsciously throwing back his broad shoulders.

Houdini bowed quietly, still with that imperturbable smile; and the crowd cheered him again, before it began slowly to dissolve.

Fig. 15. *Houdini in straitjacket on roof top edge.*

These news accounts have been quoted in detail because they give a firsthand, "on the spot" report of how the sensational Straitjacket Escape impressed the public of its time, whether a packed theater audience, or an outdoor crowd of 20,000 persons, the estimated number that witnessed Houdini's escape in Pittsburgh, a feat which he repeated in other cities from coast to coast.

From the explanation of the escape, as already given, the reader will note a surprising speed-up in the dozen years from the time it was first performed openly. From a quarter hour

Fig. 16. *Houdini suspended in straitjacket.*

of hard struggling on the stage, it had been reduced to about three minutes in midair.

In one way, hanging upside down was helpful. It made it easier for Houdini to work his arms over his head, as the action was downward, not upward. But it could mean longer and more painstaking work with the straps; and it was a mistake to prolong an outdoor escape, as it taxed both the patience of the crowd and the endurance of the performer.

Through long practice and frequent escapes from the straitjacket, Houdini had managed to cut the time considerably, but how he reduced it to such a minimum was something that baffled even magical minds until, years later, Hardeen revealed the secret that only he and Houdini had known.

In the suspended escape, Houdini used a jacket of a special type. It was a regulation straitjacket, or near enough to satisfy the persons who strapped Houdini into it. But it was designed for quick action, the secret being that the sleeves were overlong and single straps were used instead of multiple straps on neck, chest, and body.

This insured slack for the arms and enabled Houdini to do quick work with the straps. Shedding the jacket became a lot simpler and faster, too, but the escape was a legitimate one. In fact, the jacket was a standard type, but a sort best suited to a rapid escape. It would have balked the average so-called "Escape King" even if he had been allowed to try it in his own cabinet.

The Bonza Jacket

There was only one "trick" straitjacket that Houdini recommended; and then only for a very special purpose that made its use legitimate. In working trunk or box escapes, Houdini frequently allowed himself to be heavily handcuffed or securely bound with ropes, from which he also escaped.

Always, however, he faced the prospect that someone might want to strap him in a straitjacket and then nail him in the box. Now, almost any box or trunk would be too small to allow the overarm action and other freedom that was necessary with the straitjacket release. But Houdini, as the master of all escapes, had to be ready to meet any challenge.

His device, which he termed the "Bonza Jacket" was a straitjacket that could be strapped in most convincing style, because outwardly it was a regulation jacket. The trick lay in the bottom of the right sleeve, the last part of the jacket that anyone would inspect. The sleeve strap was simply hooked—not sewn or riveted—in to the end of the sleeve.

Once strapped in the jacket, it was simply a matter of finding the hook with the fingers and releasing it. The strap would then come free, releasing the arms, so the hands could work on the body straps as in the usual escape. Even the final removal of the jacket was simplified: one arm, and then the other, could be worked from the sleeves. After the escape, the strap was hooked back into the end of the sleeve.

The interesting feature of the "Bonza Jacket" is that the sleeves were necessarily shorter than those of the usual jacket, so that the fingers could reach the release. This, if anything, made the escape look more difficult, as short sleeves could not be worked over the head.

To stand a full and thorough inspection the "Bonza" had the release sewn or riveted in place. In either case it was

Fig. 17. *Soldiers tightening straitjacket.*

then as valid as any regulation jacket; in fact, escaping from it would be just as difficult, so far as the jacket itself was concerned.

The "difference" lay in a small cutting tool that was dropped into the sleeve after the jacket had been examined.

This was particularly easy in the case of the straitjacket— as opposed to other escape devices—because no one would suspect the use of such an appliance. Once his hands were encased in the sleeves, the escape artist obtained the cutter and used it to free the end of the strap.

Afterward the strap would have to be taped in place or fixed with a soft metal rivet. The "Bonza" was designed for cabinet use only, as an escape from that type of jacket could not be done in full view of the audience. That would have given away the secret of the "loose sleeve" the moment the release was made. But in working this jacket with the usual "challenge" box escape, Houdini would have used a cabinet anyway.

With some such escapes, it would be easier to pull the sleeve release; then escape from the box, by working with the hands through the cloth of the sleeve. Once out of the box, there would be more freedom in getting at the jacket straps.

The Needle Trick

JUST WHEN AND WHERE the so-called "East Indian Needle Trick" was first performed is an unanswered question, but it was Houdini who brought it from the obscurity of the Dime Museum and turned a sideshow stunt into a dramatic mystery. Houdini probably first saw it during the 1890s when he was performing at Coney Island and traveling with a circus. At any rate, he did the trick in a modern form, using packets of machine-finished needles, which first were manufactured about the year 1885.

One of the earliest references to Houdini's performance of this mystery appeared in his own *Conjurers' Monthly Magazine* for June 1908, in a report on the Fourth Annual Dinner of the Society of American Magicians, held at the Marlborough Hotel in New York City. It reads:

> Houdini then presented the mysterious Hindoo Needle Trick in which he called for a committee of two physicians from the audience. Drs. S. R. Ellison and Emil Heuel volunteered, but failed to detect how Houdini apparently swallowed fifty needles and ten yards of thread, and finally brought up the needles threaded.

The trick, however, had already been tested on physicians, if not magicians, according to an account in a biographical booklet on Houdini, which states:

In the East Indian Needle Mystery, Houdini swallows fifty to one hundred needles, twenty yards of thread and brings them all up threaded, after his mouth and throat have been examined by a committee of surgeons. In Boston, at Keith's Theatre, 1906, at a special morning performance, he performed this feat before 1600 physicians and not one could give a correct solution as to his method.

Several years passed before Houdini made the Needle Trick a regular feature in his act. When he did, it created a sensation. Here is a graphic and detailed account of its presentation on the stage of the New Cross Empire Theatre in London, May 14, 1913, where he worked it as a preliminary to the "Water Torture Cell." The review is from the *Magical World,* a popular weekly of that period:

Before a committee from the audience, Houdini introduces his East Indian Needle Trick. Two packets of "sharps" and a reel of thread are examined. The performer subjects his mouth, throat and tongue to rigid scrutiny by those on the stage; then proceeds to place bunches of the needles on his tongue and apparently swallows them, until the full contents of the two packets are consumed.

A long length of thread follows suit and the whole is washed down by a glass of water. Again, his mouth is examined before he reproduces the end of thread between his lips, which on being withdrawn discloses all the needles suspended from the cotton (thread) at regular intervals.

The feat appears all the more remarkable as it is performed after a speech of five minutes duration and without the artiste leaving the stage.

Several months later, we read another mention in the *Magical World* of a program which Houdini gave on board the steamship *Kronprinzessin Cecilie,* on July 12, 1913, wherein he featured "The Hindoo Needle Trick, the secret of which is known only to the Hindoo Yogis."

Now here, it would seem, was a closely guarded secret known only to the mystics of the Orient. It had to be just that, to baffle the best medical and magical minds of the period. Presumably, Houdini had learned the mystery when in India, or had delved deeply into the lore of yoga, to come up with something as impossible as all that.

Like many good tricks, however, it was comparatively simple, as will be evidenced from a reading of the explanation:

How to Swallow a Number of Needles
and Yards of Thread

The trick is performed as follows: In the first place, thread a dozen needles, put them in as small a compass as possible and place them between the gum and the upper lip. You can speak without difficulty and without any effort: they will remain there. Let the needles be short ones and take the end of the thread a little distance from the needles, and deposit it between the gum and the lips in such a position that you can always feel it and pull it out when required.

Thus being prepared, of course unknown to your audience, you take your second dose of needles, placing them one by one on your tongue, seeming to swallow them, but depositing them on the other side of your mouth between your gums and lip, which will effectually conceal them, notwithstanding an examination of the mouth. Afterward, roll up between your fingers about a yard of thread: place this in your mouth and with your tongue conceal it between your gum and lip.

Take a drink of water, make a few wry faces, then place your finger and thumb to your mouth, securing the end of the thread upon which the needles are threaded; draw it out and exhibit it, taking an early opportunity of retiring to get rid of the needles concealed in your mouth. This is a most effective trick and easily performed. Be careful not to swallow the needles.

What if this brief explanation had appeared in print and gained wide circulation while Houdini was featuring the Needle Trick? Would the master mystifier have gone on with it, still claiming that its secret was known only to the yogis and himself?

Certainly, Houdini would have, because he did. The explanation is taken verbatim from a dime booklet entitled *Magic Made Easy,* which appeared in 1910 and had been peddled by the thousands for three years before Houdini "opened" at the New Cross Empire. What was more, the Needle Trick had been culled along with others, from still older sources.

That meant nothing to Houdini, the way he "sold" the Needle Mystery. People just wouldn't believe that it could be done that simply.

Houdini continued to do the Needle Trick from that time on, always with the same mystifying result.

When he showed it at the New York Hippodrome, five years later, the dime books telling how the trick was done were being sold in novelty shops across Sixth Avenue, but people still paid their admission to the Hipp to have Houdini fool them with it. In performing the Needle Trick at the Hippodrome, Houdini was actually presenting the "world's smallest trick" on the "world's largest stage," a fantastic contrast to the gigantic "Vanishing Elephant" illusion that he featured in the same setting. This raises another question: How could people see the Needle Trick on such a huge stage?

Actually, they didn't see it, or at least they scarcely saw it, but Houdini's presentation was such that they didn't have to see the needles to know what was being done. His work with the committee indicated exactly what was going on, even to the "swallowing" of the needles. At the finish, when the needles were drawn out threaded, they stretched well across the stage and tiny as they were, they scintillated strikingly in the spotlight.

Houdini heightened the effect by swallowing "two" packets of needles, one after the other, thus making the trick seem doubly difficult. This also accounted for the large number of needles—approximately fifty in all—that came out threaded. Most important, however, was his manner of threading the duplicate lot.

Instead of merely being strung on the thread, the needles were knotted there at regular intervals. By tying a knot on each side of a needle, a little "play" was allowed, so that the needles were loose, as if normally threaded. But there was no danger of having them cluster together, which might have proved injurious both to the trick and the performer.

Houdini supplied the Needle Trick with certain "refinements," and most of the performers who do the trick today follow quite closely to his original routine, which ran as follows:

HOUDINI
PRESENTING THE YOGIE MASTERPIECE

Fig. 18. *"The biggest little mystery feat—the East Indian needle masterpiece, wherein Houdini swallows one hundred needles, twenty yards of thread, and brings up the needles threaded."*

First: The packets of needles that were shown to the audience. These were ordinary needles, but their points were preferably dulled to prevent any slight pricks. Houdini, who made almost a fetish of using "unfaked" items on every possible occasion, would willingly have worked the trick with needles furnished him by the committee, provided they were the right size. He was so skilled in the trick that sharp points did not bother him.

Next: The threaded needles. These were knotted as described and the amount of interval can be pretty well gauged from the specifications of the trick as Houdini presented it. Some fifty needles to thirty feet of thread allowed about six inches between needles with approximately two feet at each end of the thread.

The thread was drawn down and up beside a needle, so that the next needle came alongside the first; and so on. The heads of the needles were thus kept together and at the finish all were neatly squared up. The end of the thread was then wound around the needles and tucked through them.

A knot in the end of the thread made it easy to find.

The needles, which now formed a compact clump, were then placed in the mouth, preferably between the lower gum and cheek, say on the right side. The term "preferably" is used advisedly, because Houdini, in having his mouth examined by committees of dentists as well as physicians, had to be ready to vary his procedure when exigencies arose.

Literally, his job was to deceive these experts by what might be styled "sleight of tongue" in much the same way that he would have baffled them by sleight of hand, the purpose of course being to conceal the threaded needles at the outset of the trick and the loose needles following the finish.

This required a great deal more thought and skill than the rudimentary instructions given in the dime book. Many people could guess where duplicate needles might be hidden, without needing to read about it, but Houdini invariably convinced them that they were wrong. That was what "made" the trick. In showing his mouth, Houdini drew his upper and lower lips away from his gums and teeth. Most suspicion was directed toward the back portion above the upper gums and Houdini drew his cheeks wide with his little fingers to give a thorough view of that area.

In drawing down his lower lips and pulling the cheeks outward, his fingers came directly over the needles and thus hid them from ordinary inspection, but that was not enough for Houdini. In the course of inspection, or while repeating it for another committee man, he would reach the needles with his tongue and work them above the upper gum, which had already been examined. Later, he would bring them down to their original position between the lower gum and cheek.

Most performers would regard such manipulation sufficient, but not Houdini. He still had to convince the most skeptical as well as capable examiners and there were some who came up with the bright idea of searching Houdini's jowls with a flashlight. upper and lower gums, all in one continuous inspection.

Houdini had a way of dodging that, too, namely, by bringing the packet of threaded needles beneath his tongue, which was depressed when the gum and cheek inspection was carried out in full. Afterward, a deft move of the tongue sidled the needles down into their original hiding place beside the lower gum, where everyone by then was satisfied that they could not be. In this placement, the heads of the needles were kept toward the front of the mouth.

All was now ready for the swallowing of the loose needles. These were placed on the extended tongue, with the heads of the needles toward the back. Houdini closed his mouth, gave a swallowing motion, and with it, tongued the loose needles between gum and cheek on the opposite side from the threaded batch. This was repeated with another packet of loose needles. Generally the needles were placed beside the upper gum as they were already on the tongue, so a lift was the quickest and least observable action. However, there were times when the lower placement was preferable and Houdini was quite as deft at transferring the loose needles as the threaded. Actually, as soon as the needles became moistened with saliva, they tended to adhere, so that the tongue could manipulate them quite readily.

The bunched-up thread, next placed on the tongue, was pushed between gum and cheek in the same fashion, though if need be, it could actually be swallowed. That was one reason why Houdini took a drink of water to "wash down" the needles and thread. If he foresaw a rigid inspection coming as an aftermath, there was no good reason to be bothered with a ball of thread along with a batch of needles.

In any case, after the swallowing action, Houdini was ready for the real climax. He brought the threaded needles on to his tongue, reached his thumb and forefinger between his lips, found the knotted end of the wound-up thread and drew it out. That end was given to a committee man, who held it while Houdini drew slowly away, letting the needles unwind on his tongue. The committee man was previously admonished not to pull on the thread, so that Houdini actually drew it taut between the needles as he moved backward, bringing needles from between his lips, one by one, each needle emerging eye first.

This was the most important point of the trick, or rather the evasion of the point, where each needle was concerned.

In working before a small group—such as physicians or magicians—Houdini often backed down the center aisle, leaving a string of threaded needles extending up to the platform. Before a larger audience, as in a theater, Houdini backed across the stage, drawing out the threaded needles as he went.

Usually Houdini presented the Needle Trick as part of a bigger act, so the examination of his mouth after the trick was almost a minor routine. The bringing out of the threaded needles after an exhaustive preliminary inspection was convincing enough, to committee as well as audience in general. But before special groups, under what amounted to test conditions, Houdini often had to convince some die-hard skeptics that his mouth was really empty, both before and after. This meant that he sometimes found it necessary to obtain the threaded needles in his mouth *after* a thorough examination had proved it to be actually empty.

Similarly, it was sometimes necessary to dispose of the ordinary needles following the trick, so that an overly skeptical committee could make a later inspection. Houdini was ready for that situation, too.

Among methods of secretly obtaining the threaded needles, here is one that was definitely known to Houdini, though there is no record of when or how often he may have employed it. The mouth was thoroughly examined and found absolutely empty, the performer raising his tongue to show nothing beneath and finally depressing his tongue with the blade of a table knife so that the inspection could be extended to his upper gums. Only after that did he proceed with the trick.

The threaded needles, in this case, were strongly magnetized. Instead of being in the performer's mouth at the outset, they were attached beneath the steel blade of the table knife, which was handy on the table.

When the inspection of the performer's mouth neared the final stage, he picked up the table knife and pressed his tongue down with the blade, holding it there, while his gums were checked.

The needles then were between the blade and the tongue. When the inspection was completed, the mouth was closed and the knife drawn from between the lips, which retained the threaded needles, the tongue immediately thrusting them between the gum and cheek.

The disposal of the ordinary needles following the trick was accomplished—when necessary—with the aid of the glass of water. Houdini always had this ruse in readiness, though he seldom needed it. When he took a swallow of water to "wash down" the needles and thread, he would toss his head back in a dramatic way that captured full attention.

So if he wanted to get rid of the loose needles afterward, he simply took another drink of water in the same way. This time, he would have the needles ready at his lips and eject them into the glass as he lowered it. His head toss would divert attention while his cupped hand hid the action. The needles would sink unnoticed to the bottom of the glass, which was promptly taken by an assistant .

No special glass was needed, as it is very difficult to notice needles at the bottom of a glass of water. They take up very little space, reflections help to conceal them, and in a glass with any frosting or ornamentation, detection is impossible.

The Needle Switch

This is an alternate method of working the Needle Trick that was known to Houdini at the time he made a feature of the mystery, but it is doubtful that he ever used it in a regular stage performance. It was useful to have in reserve, however, to nonplus a difficult committee.

The presentation was very similar to that of the usual Needle Trick, but with this exception: Instead of "swallowing" needles and thread separately, the thread was openly wound about a batch of examined needles and the lot was placed in the mouth as one. Almost immediately, the thread could be drawn out with the needles strung along it, the mystery again being how they could have attained that state.

Two batches of needles were used, but the threaded group was not hidden in the mouth. Instead, they were wrapped in their thread and tucked beneath a finger ring on the inside of the finger of the left hand.

The ordinary needles were shown when taken from their packet and a thread was wrapped about them, exactly as with the duplicate set. All during the procedure the back of the left hand was kept toward the audience so that the threaded needles could not be seen.

When about to place the needles in his mouth, the performer held them at the tip of his left thumb and forefinger. The right hand approached to take the needles, but drew up the duplicates from the finger ring instead. All in the same move, the left thumb and fingers let the originals fall into the left palm.

Without a moment's hesitation, the right hand openly placed the needles and thread on the tongue. A swallowing motion followed, and it was simply a case of reaching into the month and drawing out the threaded needles. The left hand disposed of the other set later.

While this lacks the "step-by-step" procedure of Houdini's regular Needle Trick and is therefore less dramatic than his "East Indian" mystery, it is very deceptive. At the same time it is a safe way of working the trick, as only the threaded set goes into the mouth and then but briefly, as the needles are drawn out almost immediately and there is no need of concealing anything in the mouth, "before" or "after."

It was from this version of the needle trick that magicians later developed the more modern mystery of the threaded razor blades.

The Threaded Razor Blades

In this presentation, the performer shows a dozen or more safety razor blades of the double-edged variety and proves their sharpness by cutting a piece of cardboard with one of the blades.

He then gathers them very carefully into a little packet which he places on a handkerchief.

Next, the magician gathers up a five-foot length of thread, which he places on his tongue and swallows with the aid of a drink of water. The razor blades go next; they are placed openly on the tongue and apparently swallowed, too.

Then, reaching into his mouth, the wizard finds an end of the string and draws it slowly into sight. Coming along with it are the razor blades, strung at intervals on the thread. Afterward, the mouth is shown to be entirely empty, proving that the loose blades must have strung themselves in some weird way.

There are two sets of blades used in the trick and one set is specially prepared, by dulling the edges beforehand. This set is threaded, so to speak, by tying blades to the thread, one by one, about twice their length apart.

The thread is doubled in between the blades and each end of the thread is tied squarely against a blade, so there are no loose ends. The idea here is to prevent the thread from being seen when the blades are in their stacked condition.

If bright steel blades are used, a white thread will be unnoticeable, while with blue blades, a dark or black thread will pass muster: the choice is governed by the type of blades used. The other set of blades can all be sharp ones; but rather than handle such risky items, many performers prefer to dull them, too, with the exception of one odd blade which is left on top of the stack for demonstration purposes.

One more item is required: an ordinary handkerchief. This is folded into quarters and laid on the table, with an open edge toward the rear. The threaded blades are placed in a stack between the folds of the handkerchief.

In performing the trick, the loose blades are first exhibited; in fact, they may be taken from a regular package. They are stacked and laid, rather gingerly, on the handkerchief, toward the folded edge at the front. A sharp blade—or the only one, if a single "sharp" is used—is taken and the cutting power of its edges is demonstrated with a piece of cardboard. It is then added to its stack.

Now, in moving the handkerchief aside, the performer flips over the open edge of the handkerchief, dropping it toward the front. This covers the stack of ordinary blades and reveals the threaded stack instead. No one suspects the exchange because the trick is still in its early stages.

The maneuver, too, is covered nicely, as the hand promptly picks up a spool of thread which is lying close by.

From this, the performer takes off a length of thread. He bunches it up, places it on his tongue and does a swallowing action, pushing the wad of thread over into the side of the mouth below the gum. Next, he picks up the stack of razor blades, places it on his tongue, closes his mouth and makes a pretense of swallowing it.

This stack is the one that is already threaded, so the trick is ready for the climax. The performer reaches into his mouth, draws the top blade from the dulled, threaded stack, and brings it out carefully, in endwise fashion from between his lips. Then, blade by blade, he continues the process, using both hands, one gripping the end blade, the other helping to bring out the others until the entire lot is shown strung between both hands.

There is little need to go into a thorough inspection of the mouth when performing this novel trick as the size of the blades is in itself impressive and seems to preclude the use of duplicates. However, the trick is "made to order" for any examination of the mouth as no extra blades are concealed there. Only the wadded thread is left afterward, and it is easy to hide, as in the Needle Trick, by keeping it at the side of the lower gum and pressing the little finger over it, when showing the mouth empty.

As an alternative, the thread may be disposed of by ejecting it into the glass when taking a drink of water immediately after the trick.

Houdini's Box Escapes

By "Box Escapes" Houdini referred most frequently to those involving wooden boxes, whether simple packing cases or those of stronger construction. Wooden boxes were sometimes wired, banded, or even lined with metal, adding to the problems of escape, all of which figured in Houdini's calculations.

There were other boxes of special or permanent construction which included those made of glass, metal, or both. These came more under the head of chests, caskets, trunks, or even cells that demanded special measures for Houdini to extricate himself from them. These types of "boxes" are discussed separately and individually.

Houdini worked three types of Box Escapes with wooden boxes of the packing case variety: First, an escape from a submerged box lowered into a river; second, a challenge escape from a box supplied by the builders; third, an escape in which a box of his own was used, but subjected to thorough and rigid examination.

Many ordinary packing boxes could be fixed so an escape was an easy matter, and Houdini could accept such boxes for a submerged escape as well as a challenge on the stage of the theater. At times he combined the two notions by having a challenge box submerged in a tank of water on the stage itself, not just at the New York Hippodrome, which had a miniature "lake" large enough to float a real ship, but at other theaters as required.

But usually the "overboard box" was an outdoor attraction intended to lure the multitudes to the theater. Its great difference from the "challenge box" was that escape from the box while under water had to be quick as well as sure.

Houdini's own notes described this version of the "Underwater Box Escape."

The Underwater Box Escape

Simple and effective in construction, this box, which resembled a common packing case, had four boards in each side and end, with a bottom of similar construction, all very solid and examinable. The top was in the form of a flat lid which was placed on the box after Houdini was in it, and was nailed solidly in place.

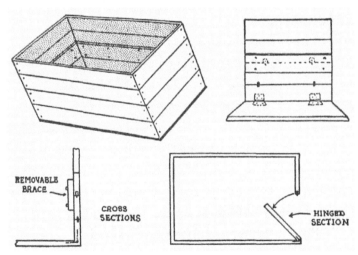

Fig. 19. *Appearance and construction of the box used in the escape from under water.*

The box was provided with air holes in the sides, ends, and bottom; these were small and obviously had no direct bearing on the escape, though they played a secondary part, as will be seen.

Ordinarily, Houdini needed air holes in order to breathe if his escape proved difficult and took longer than expected. With the "Underwater Escape," if Houdini didn't appear within three or four minutes after the box went overboard, it would have to be hauled up in a hurry.

The holes were necessary, however, when the box was submerged in order that it would fill with water and sink more rapidly. Otherwise the box would have remained too buoyant, even with the heavy metal weights attached to it. Suspense was rife from the moment the box disappeared below the surface, with people counting not just minutes but seconds, until Houdini bobbed into sight and swam to the boat or wharf from which the box had been lowered and there clambered on board.

Now for the manner of this quick escape, as Houdini himself designed it:

Of the four boards making up one end of the box, the two lower ones were fastened together as a single unit, but they were not nailed to the sides of the box. Any nails that showed there were simply short, or faked. Nor was that lower pair of end boards nailed to the bottom of the box.

Instead, the lower board of the pair was fastened to the bottom of the box by concealed interior hinges, so that the pair of boards formed a "trap" which was made to open inward, allowing sufficient space for Houdini to slide out quite easily, as the box itself was oversized.

So that the box could stand inspection before and after

the escape, the upper board of the trap had two automatic catches which fitted into grooves or slots in the edge of the board just above. This fitted so closely that the joint could not be seen; but with a thin steel wedge Houdini pushed back the catches and released the trap by pulling it in toward him. That was where the air holes served, as they enabled him to gain a finger grip. Once outside, he pulled the trap outward in the same manner, the catches springing back into place.

In his notes, Houdini suggested hiding the interior joint by having slats or braces running around the middle of the box. These made the box look stronger, but by smuggling a small screwdriver into the box Houdini was able to remove the inner brace before the box reached the water; thus he could get at the catches.

From the outside, the trap would be pulled shut as usual, but the brace would be left loose inside the box.

No one noticed this when the box was hauled up, as the top was still nailed on it.

Special Free Test

Sunday, July 7 at 11 a. m.

Pier 6, East River
One block from South Ferry

HARRY HOUDINI

securely handcuffed and leg ironed will be placed in a heavy packing case, which will be nailed and roped, then encircled by steel bands firmly nailed. Two hundred pounds of iron weights will then be lashed to this box containing HOUDINI, the box will then BE THROWN INTO THE EAST RIVER. HOUDINI will undertake to release himself whilst submerged under water.

The Most Daring Feat ever attempted in this or any other age.

SUNDAY RAIN or SHINE

Fig. 20

Fig. 21. *Houdini being lowered into the East River in a box.*

But in that case, Houdini's assistants had to remove the box from the scene and put the brace back in place before allowing anyone to examine the box again.

The Challenge Box Escape

The same type of box could be used on the stage of a theater, with Houdini effecting his escape inside a cabinet. In this case, he had all the time he wanted, so if he used the box with the inner brace, he was able to put it back in place from the outside. That sounds impossible, but Houdini had two ways of doing it. One was to have the brace held to the box with screws from the outside as well as from the inside. That should have made it doubly difficult. Instead, it solved the problem, because:

The screws on the inside were long ones, running through the brace into the solid planking. Those on the outside were short, that went part way through the boards but did not reach the brace. When Houdini took out the long screws from the inside, the brace came loose.

Once he opened the trap, Houdini—still inside the box— put the brace back on the trap half, using the long screws. In the other screw holes, which connected the brace with the solid portion of the end, he put short screws. He then emerged from the box and drew the trap shut, the brace coming into place with it.

Houdini would then replace the short screws in the outside of the box with long ones that went clear through into the brace itself. The box, when examined afterward, would be more solid than at the start!

Usually, to serve for "challenge" purposes, a box had to be the sort that could be "gaffed" or altered after it had been built to specifications and supplied by the challengers. Otherwise, it became more of a "standard" box escape, utilizing the performer's own equipment.

One type, which could be planned as a "challenge" box but was better suited to the "standard" escape routine, was described by Houdini as the slide-up box.

The Slide-Up Box

This type of box was strongly constructed of boards set in an upright framework which formed the corner posts and the outer rim at the top of the box. The corners were in the form of angles and the lid of the box was reinforced with braces, being just large enough to be nailed to the top boards of the box proper; not the surrounding rim that topped the posts.

If put together neatly and held with screws, not nails, such a box could be "tricked" quite readily. Again, the "long" and "short" principle applied where the screws were concerned. A few long screws were used to secure the inner section of the box to the corner posts and these were inserted from the inside of the box.

All the screws that ran from the outside, that is, through the posts and into the box, were short screws. The same applied to those inserted up through the bottom; they were also too short to reach the walls of the box proper. Once inside, Houdini only had to remove the long screws and the box could be slid straight up from the frame. Since the top was nailed only to the box proper; it went up with it.

When Houdini stood up, the box rose too, giving him space to emerge between the posts. With a tight-

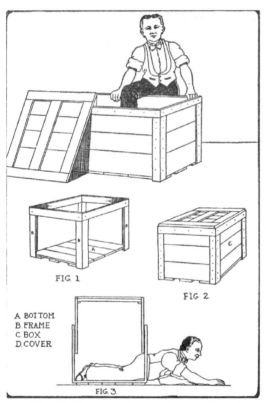

A BOTTOM
B. FRAME
C BOX
D. COVER

FIG. 1

FIG 2

FIG. 3.

Fig. 22. *Construction and operation of the slide-up box.*

fitting box, it was unnecessary to have any long screws inside, as no one could lift the inner box except Houdini, when he was nailed inside it. Then his weight held down the bottom while his powerful shoulders supplied the needed leverage to push the box loose. Once he was out, he could use short screws from the outside to replace the inside long screws that had been removed. Then, the long screws could be used to replace the short ones going from the outside in.

By having the top frame attached to the inner section of the box instead of the posts, it was possible to nail on a full-sized cover, as the frame itself would go up with the box.

Another interesting form was the metal-rimmed box.

The Metal-Rimmed Box

Here no posts were needed because the corners of what appeared to be an ordinary wooden packing case were bound with angle-shaped strips of metal. These ran along the top edge, down the corners of the box, and finally along the bottom edge of the box. All along were nails to hold the rim firmly in place, the box itself being well nailed together.

With Houdini inside the box, a precise fitted lid was placed on top and the metal edge bent over it, being hammered flat and nailed in place so that the box was positively secure at the top. Yet escape was swift, despite these seemingly impossible conditions.

The box was made in two separate sections, the top row of boards fitting on the rest, with pins and sockets keeping it firmly in position. The metal rim was nailed to the lower section, but the lower part was free and provided with dummy nail heads. There were heavy cleats at the lower corners of the box; the upright portions of the rim slid down beneath them. The lower or bottom rim was actually attached to the bottom edge of the box, giving the impression that the metalwork formed a complete and solid frame. But by pushing up the top, Houdini could lift the upper section, together with all the metal rim except the part that girded the bottom edge.

A slide-up box of this type could have a metal lining as well; this being firmly nailed or screwed to the bottom and lower

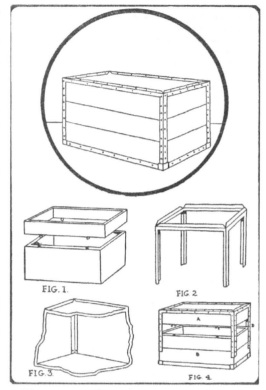

FIG. 1.

FIG 2

FIG. 3.

FIG 4.

Fig. 23. *Details of the metal-rimmed box.*

section of the box; but with fake nail or screw heads where the upper portion was concerned. With such a lining coming clear to the top edge of the box, the box was all the firmer, but the push-up would work the same.

Houdini used a metal-lined box with some of his milk can escapes, the milk can—containing Houdini— being inside the box, which had a lid that could be rapidly locked in place. The box worked on a slide-up principle similar to those just described, enabling Houdini to make a quick escape by pushing up the top of the can and top of the box in one action.

The Iron Box Challenge

This escape is made from a box of solid iron, the corners and the sides being riveted in place. The cover of the box is also made of iron and fits down over the box itself. Designed as a challenge, this box can be made by any manufacturer or under the auspices of any group of challengers. The box is exactly what it appears to be: a large box of iron that will withstand almost any amount of pressure or hammering. The box itself has no device for locking. It must contain air holes in the top, as usual in escape devices, and a large hole is drilled in each side near the upper edge, with corresponding holes in the cover.

The accompanying sketch provides for four of these holes; one in each side, the box being nearly cubical in shape, and large enough to contain the performer, with allowance for space in which to move. The method of fastening the cover on the box is also convincing. Four solid bolts are used, each

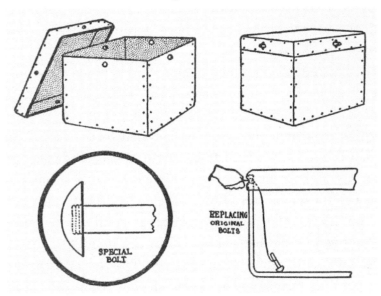

Fig. 24. *Details of the iron box challenge.*

with a large head; these bolts fit into the holes in the sides of the box. The bolts are pushed through from the inside, and the ends that protrude have holes in them so that padlocks may be attached. The box and the bolts are placed on exhibition and anyone may satisfy himself that this escape must be impregnable, first because of the strength of the material used, second, because of the size and solidity of the bolts. The bolts must necessarily be large so as to allow for holes of sufficient size to receive the padlocks.

When the escape is to be made, the box is brought on the stage; the performer enters it, and the bolts are inserted by the committee members. Then the lid is pressed down on the box; the bolts are pushed through, and the padlocks are attached. There is no possible way for the performer to reach the locks; they are large and of standard pattern, examined or supplied by the challengers. Apparently the performer is in the box to stay. The box is covered with the cabinet, and several minutes pass; then the curtain opens and the escapist steps out. There is the box, the padlocks still on the bolts.

Everything is examined inside and outside, and all is found to be in regular order. The artifice by which this escape is accomplished is very simple. It depends on the method by which the cover is fastened to the box, a plan which is specially suited to be of aid to the performer. The only way to hold the cover to the box is by bolts through the holes. This seems fair enough because the bolts are made of iron, like the box, and are of simple, solid construction.

The head of the bolts must be on the inside, so that the locks can be attached on the outside. The heads of the bolts are quite as strong as the box itself, but when the cover is placed on the box, the bolts must be drawn in to allow it to pass. This is done by the performer. When the cover is fitted in place, he pushes the bolts back again.

That is what the committee men believe he does; actually, when he draws in the bolts, he pulls them all the way in and lays them on the floor of the box.

The Plate Glass Box

Concealed on his person are four fake bolts, exactly resembling the genuine ones; and these bolts are the ones he pushes out. The difference between the fake bolts and the genuine bolts is this: the fake bolts have heads that unscrew. They are made in two pieces instead of one. As soon as the cabinet is closed over the box, the performer unscrews the heads from the fake bolts, draws them in, and pushes out the free ends. The bolts fall with the padlocks, and the performer is free to lift the cover of the box. The notes on this escape show short chains attached from the box to the padlocks; these serve the ostensible purpose of keeping the padlocks permanently attached to the box; their actual use is to prevent the bolts and padlocks from clattering to the floor when they are pushed out.

The method of replacing the bolts is not given in the notes on this escape, but this detail is not difficult to supply. By using large holes in the box and cover, strings may be attached to the genuine bolts and passed through the holes in the box and the cover. When the cover is replaced on the box, the strings are drawn, pulling the bolts out again. Then the padlocks are picked or unlocked and are transferred from the fake bolts to the real ones.

The escape from a box made of sheets of plate glass was performed by both Houdini and Mrs. Houdini. It is an interesting and unusual escape, as the performer, when imprisoned, is visible from every angle. The box is of simple construction. The sides are held together by metal angles; these are held in place by heavy bolts which pass through holes drilled in the glass and in the angles. The bolts are very tight; the heads are on the inside; hence the nuts cannot be undone by anyone who is imprisoned in the box. There are two angles for each pair of connecting edges. The cover of the box—also a sheet of plate glass—lies flat on the top of the box proper, and is hinged to one of the long sides of the box. Three hinges are used; they are held in place with bolts, just as the angles are kept in position.

The use of three hinges makes the cover fit exactly. The front side of the box has two hinged hasps at the upper edge; the top has two metal staples projecting up at the front edge, held by tight bolts and nuts.

When the performer enters the box, the cover is closed; the hasps are folded down on the top, and large, heavy padlocks are slipped through the staples. The glass box may be thoroughly examined. Washers are used with the bolts in order to protect the glass, but there is no deception about them. The fact that plate glass is used makes any hidden mechanism an impossibility. Any person can satisfy himself that the box is without preparation, and an inspection can be made in a very few minutes. Yet the performer escapes from the crystal casket a few minutes after the cabinet is placed over it, and the box is found to be firmly locked as ever.

The secret of the escape lies in the hinges. These are not faked, but the bolts through the back of the box are of special construction. Each bolt is large and consists of two portions, the bolt itself, which is hollow at one end, and the bolthead, which is provided with a small screw-bolt. When the bolt-head is screwed into the hollow end of the bolt (which is threaded to receive it), the result is apparently a solid bolt that exactly resembles the real bolts used on all the other parts of the glass box. From inside the box, the performer can unscrew the boltheads, push the bolts out of the holes, lift up the cover with the hasps acting as hinges, and thus make an escape.

So that the bolts may pass the most rigid inspection, the heads are screwed in so tightly that they cannot be removed except by the use of a special tool. One method of accomplishing this is with bolts that have small holes in the solid

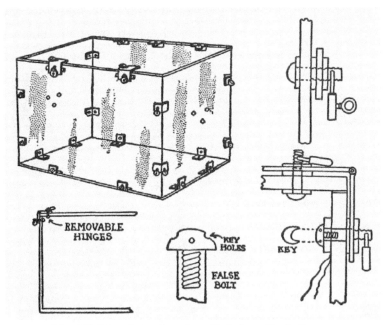

Fig. 25. *The plate glass box. Note how the bolts are locked, the diagrams show construction of the false bolts.*

heads. The holes are short depressions that do not extend deep into the heads. The performer has a flat key, with extending prongs, which are pushed into the holes of each bolthead; the key is turned, and the bolthead is quickly and easily unscrewed. After the escape, the replacement of the special bolts is not a difficult matter.

The heads are put back in place, and the nuts are removed. The bolts may be attached to cords which are passed through the holes in the glass so that the bolts may be drawn into position from within the box and the nuts replaced. But if the padlocks are the performer's own or are of a type which may be easily opened, the simplest method is to unlock them, releasing the front of the cover, and thus replaces the bolts in the hinges.

The cover may then be closed and relocked. Another method is to tilt the box backward, slip the bolts through the holes in the back, and fit the hinges over the ends of the bolt s, after which the nuts may be tightened from the outside.

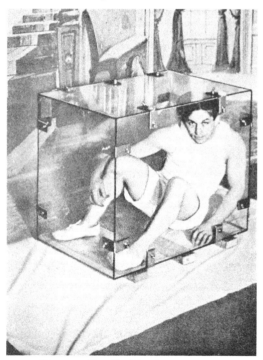

It is quite an easy matter to substitute genuine bolts for the special bolts after the escape. The extra bolts may be concealed in the cabinet.

This will allow the glass box to be examined with no possibility of anyone's

Fig. 26. *Houdini in the glass box.*

discovering the secret. The only article which the performer must carry into the box is the small flat key, which may be concealed without any difficulty. There are no less than forty-two bolts used in the plate glass box. These are all alike in appearance and all but three of them are genuine. With so many bolts to examine, and without the special tool at their disposal, the committee men have no opportunity to discover anything amiss. Suspicious committee men naturally direct their attention to the hasps and staples of the box. The bolts used are genuine; that is a subtle feature of the trick. Opening the cover from the hinge side is an excellent procedure. The plate glass box is an ingenious escape, because its secret is so effectively protected. It is quickly and easily accomplished and affords no complications and is convincing to both the audience and the committee because of the simple construction of the box, which permits a view of the interior after the box is closed.

The Spanish Maiden Escape

The escape from the Spanish Maiden was evidently part of Houdini's scheme to produce some day a scene in which the stage would be filled with strange relics of ancient inquisitions, from any one of which he could effect an escape! The Spanish Maiden, a modification of the famous instrument of torture, is a box that stands upright with a hinged section that opens outward. It is shaped roughly like the human body, and the front is painted to resemble a maiden. Both parts of the box are alike—the box proper and the cover—and the interior of each section is lined with spikes. In this detail it differs from the ancient Iron Maiden, for whereas the spikes were arranged so as to pierce the person imprisoned within, those of the modernized device merely surround the prisoner so that it is impossible for him to move freely. When the Maiden is closed, padlocks may be attached to staples in order to make escape apparently impossible.

There are three padlocks; the iron bands to which they are attached pass around the Spanish Maiden and terminate in the hinges.

The secret of the escape from the Spanish Maiden lies in hinges, which are specially made. They are pin hinges, but each pin is cut like a ratchet on one side, and two springs inside the tube hold the pin in position. When the box is open, the pins cannot be removed from the hinges because the lower spring swings around with the hinge engages a groove in the opposite side of the pin. Any attempt to pull the pin upward will fail. When the Spanish Maiden is closed, both springs engage the ratchet; the upper spring is designed to raise the pin from the hinge, the lower spring to keep the pin from falling. By gripping one of the spikes at the hinge side of the cover (or front section of the box) the performer can lift the cover upward a fraction of an inch. The looseness of the padlocks permits this. Each time he lifts up and releases, the upper spring of each hinge works on the ratchet in the pin, and thus the pins are gradually forced out of the springs.

When the operation has been completed, the pins are clear of the hinges and the performer opens the box at that side, the padlocks serving as hinges. After the escape, the performer replaces the pins by pushing them up through the hinges from the bottom. Everything is secure once more, and the spiked box may be inspected by the committee. When the box is closed, no one will detect the ingenious method of removing the pins from the hinges; when it is opened, the pins cannot be removed. Hence the mode of escape is indetectable, for it is workable only by the person who is confined inside.

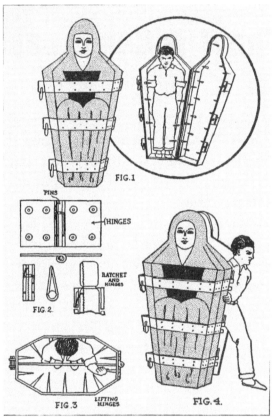

Fig. 27. *The escape from the Spanish Maiden.*

The Milk Can Escape

IN A CERTAIN SENSE the "Milk Can Escape" can be rated as one of Houdini's greatest, for it enabled him to get away from the endless round of jailbreaks and handcuff challenges that had limited his career and confronted him with a hotbed of competition.

Anyone could call himself a "Handcuff King," but to pose as "another Houdini" would have been an infringement of a name. By identifying a sensational escape with himself, Houdini was able to shake off imitators. So the Milk Can Escape, as it came to be known, actually marked Houdini's emergence from a field that had become so overcrowded that it was being relegated to the commonplace.

The Milk Can Escape did not supplant Houdini's challenges. Instead, it gave them new impact, forcing them to more sensational levels in order to compare with the Milk Can. Later Houdini was to produce more elaborate mysteries, such as his Water Torture Cell, Walking Through a Brick Wall, and the Living Burial; but the Milk Can Escape may rightfully be regarded as the stepping-stone to these newer sensations.

How well the Milk Can Escape "stood up" when audience tested is evidenced by the fact that Houdini first featured it early in 1908; then after a few seasons it was also presented regularly by his brother Hardeen, who, as Houdini's successor, performed the escape in his last show on May 30, 1945, some thirty-eight years after it was introduced.

During those years the Milk Can had undergone some changes, various models having been produced, but to the public eye, the Houdini Milk Can looked exactly the same and as baffling as ever, its simple, solid construction apparently rendering it escape proof.

That, plus the fact that the escape was made while the can was filled with water, made the effect sensational indeed.

For years Houdini had been trying to devise an escape that would incorporate the underwater feature with that of a challenge, but without avail. Trunks and packing boxes were formidable, but not watertight; tanks and boilers were too cumbersome and heavy. Besides, all such items lacked the stamp of individuality that the device required to distinguish it as Houdini's own.

Tracing the Milk Can to its source is a neat problem in itself, even for someone well acquainted both with Houdini and his times. Among his challenges, Houdini had occasionally escaped from huge wooden milk churns supplied by local dairies, but he had always specified that air holes be bored in them, as with a packing case.

Houdini had also been doing boiler escapes as challenges and the idea of a cylindrical container that would be both airtight and liquid-tight apparently stemmed from that, for during the week of December 17, 1907 he introduced an escape from a galvanized iron liquid air can at the Majestic Theater in Chicago. At the same time, the audience was "informed" that this "challenge" was a "mechanical problem," the first that Houdini had ever presented.

Otherwise interpreted, Houdini was simply sounding out his public to learn if they would accept a contrivance of his own construction as willingly as some device provided by local artisans. Apparently they did, for the Milk Can Escape soon followed.

Whether the liquid air can was converted directly into the milk can is a moot question, but it is likely that one led to the other. Possibly the liquid air can was simply a "throw-off" so that no one would know that Houdini actually had the milk can in mind. For the Milk Can, when it did appear, made much more sense than the liquid air container. It was better even than a milk churn, for milk cans were a common sight on railway platforms throughout the Midwest and around every farmyard.

These cans were of small capacity—ten gallons or so—or they would have been too difficult to load when filled with milk for shipment to the city.

But it took no great imagination on an audience's part to accept a man-sized milk can simply as a mammoth version of the ordinary article and quite as normal. It was so familiar an object that there was no reason to regard it with undue suspicion. Capable of standing rigid examination by a committee from the audience, the giant milk can proved as effective as any challenge, but with the advantage that no local outfit could come in with one of their own, because they just weren't made that big.

Even if anyone had gone to the trouble and expense of building a special milk can as a challenge, Houdini could have turned it down on the ground that it was a nonregulation item. So the sensational new escape was an immediate hit, even though the proportions of Houdini's giant milk can differed from those of its smaller prototype.

The small commercial milk can was simply an upright cylinder, running from a solid bottom up to a top rim or "shoulder," where it slanted inward and upward to a much narrower cylinder which formed a "collar" that was topped by a flanged metal cap. Since the milk can was used simply for pouring liquid in and out, the "neck" or "collar" could naturally be small.

But with the oversized Milk Can, the neck had to be large enough for Houdini to get in, which called for a much larger interior than necessary, adding to its bulk and weight. Houdini compromised by constructing a milk can with slightly tapering sides from shoulder down to bottom. This made the neck as wide in diameter as the bottom, but the still wider shoulder gave the contrivance its "milk can" look. What was even more important, it allowed Houdini to fake the device to his own liking, assuring a speedy exit. To appreciate its effect on the audience, however, we must describe the Milk Can Escape as he presented it.

Houdini opened his act with some preliminary escapes, among them the Straitjacket release, which until the advent of the Milk Can Escape, was his most sensational number. Having conditioned his audience for the grand finale, he then called on the committee to inspect the milk can, which was brought on stage for that purpose.

There it was, a rather ominous device, almost monstrous in appearance. While the committee members were tapping it, peering inside it, studying its simple yet formidable construction, Houdini's assistants were bringing on pails of water, making its purpose all too plain. Houdini retired from the stage in the meantime and climaxed the situation when he reappeared, attired in a bathing suit, ready to enter the examined milk can which even now his assistants were filling to the brim with water.

The milk can, squatty in shape, came only a little more than waist high to Houdini. When he nimbly entered it and suddenly dipped from sight, the audience gasped a prolonged "Aaahh!" as though something phenomenal had already been accomplished.

That wasn't in the original script; it was something that Houdini chanced on almost accidentally. Because of its jutting shoulder, the milk can had an interior bulge like that of the famed Indian Basket, which seems scarcely large enough to contain the boy who disappears from within it.

Fig. 28. *Houdini in a milk can.*

So the audience was won at the very outset.

The people sat breathless while Houdini was deep within the confines of the metal monster, realizing that he too was breathless, but in a more realistic way.

When informed of this by his assistants, who were trained to observe the audience reactions, Houdini took advantage of the dramatic possibilities, staying under water to his limit during that first try, all as a build up to the greater suspense that was to follow.

When Houdini emerged from the initial test, the milk can was again filled to its capacity with water pouring over its brim. Once more Houdini plunged into the depths and assistants hurriedly clashed in more water, to make up for splashings. Then, still more speedily, the already examined cap was clamped to the top of the milk can and padlocks were inserted to fasten the half dozen hasps firmly to their staples.

Swiftly, the cabinet was dropped over the milk can and the curtained front drawn tight. The orchestra worked up to a frenzied tempo, while the audience and the committee waited with bated breath. Minutes passed, beyond the allotted time limit until, when the endurance limit, too, seemed reached, the front curtain whipped open and Houdini emerged dripping with water, the milk can standing padlocked and intact behind him, awaiting further examination.

With such an act, it was small wonder that Houdini was on his way to new fame and fortune. Soon he was heading the bill over a big-time vaudeville circuit, although the manager had reportedly said that he wanted acts that carried at least three people and closed with a big illusion and that handcuff acts would be relegated to the five- and ten-cent houses.

Actually, the Milk Can Escape put Houdini's act into the required category, since it rated as a stage illusion. He also carried the specified number of assistants and opened with a straitjacket in preference to handcuffs, so there may have been some truth to the statement, although Houdini vehemently disputed it.

By August 1908, Houdini was on his way to Europe, where he featured the Milk Can Escape during the next three years, making a particular hit in the British music halls, where his act was billed as "The Impossible Possible" and was augmented by individual challenges.

Now for an explanation of the possible "impossibility," as the Milk Can Escape was appropriately heralded:

The shape of the can, as well as giving it a "normal" look, helped to draw suspicion from its real secret. People naturally suspected trickery in the top or figured that some complex mechanism was built into the can itself.

About the last thing they considered was the shoulder, which was where the answer lay in the original milk can.

The shoulder was composed of a solid metal band, which was ostensibly riveted to the upper rim of the milk can proper. Actually, the rivet heads were dummies that did not continue through. False rivet ends were placed inside, so that the more thorough the examination, the more convinced the committee would become that the contrivance was a solid, genuinely riveted article.

The only way to disprove that fact was to dislodge the upper section of the trick can, which they never managed to do for the good but simple reason that it was too tightly jammed in place. That raises another question: How did Houdini force the top portion from the milk can, if the committee couldn't? The answer was that Houdini worked from the inside; not the outside. Once confined within the milk can, he was able to supply a powerful upward thrust against the slant between the shoulder and the neck, literally "breaking" the upper section free. This could not be done from the outside, as it would be impossible to gain a good enough grip to pull the milk can apart.

Even if an ambitious committee man had clambered into the milk can when it was brought on stage, he couldn't have forced it open from within. Such efforts would have caused the milk can to wobble and perhaps overturn.

Again, a question: Then how could Houdini risk it when the milk can was filled with water, limiting the time of his escape to a few minutes at most?

In this case, the answer was in the water itself. As well as representing a danger, it furnished additional weight, enough of it to anchor the milk can solidly to the stage so that Houdini, to quote his own description, could "force the gag so as to get out."

Once out, Houdini replaced the upper section of the milk can. ramming it down so firmly that it would again stand thorough inspection by the committee.

Here he was aided and abetted by the

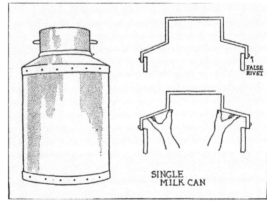

Fig. 29. *Diagram of escape from a single milk can.*

orchestra, which played loudly enough to drown the sound of hammering within the cabinet, where the audience supposed that Houdini was drowning inside the very milk can which, at that moment, he was putting back into its proper shape.

This introduced an element of suspense quite different from that found in most of Houdini's stage escapes. Hitherto, the emphasis had been on the difficulties provided by the restraint itself, rather than the time factor. In some instances, the longer the escape took—whether from ropes, manacles, packing case, or metal box—the greater its audience appeal became.

People often waited patiently for a half hour or longer until Houdini emerged triumphant from his cabinet to conclude a regulation escape or challenge. But with the milk can, tension mounted much more rapidly. If Houdini hadn't come out within five minutes at the most, it could have been taken for granted that he wouldn't be coming out at all.

This meant that there could be no stalling with the milk can, otherwise there would not have been time to "set" the contrivance after the escape had been effected. However, Houdini's stay in the milk can was not limited to the time he could hold his breath; actually, he was able to obtain air immediately after the cover of the milk can was clamped in place.

In immersing himself in the milk can, Houdini did so with such vehemence that enough water overflowed to create a sizable air space in the neck of the can. That, plus the fact that the cover itself was curved, allowed him to tilt his face upward and obtain a fresh breath of air before he started the escape. True, the assistants went through a routine of pouring additional water into the milk can after Houdini was inside it, as if they were filling it clear to the brim; but this was done in a great hurry, as others were waiting to put the lid in place, so in the final analysis, there was more splashing than anything else.

Oddly, the overflow was an important factor with the early model milk can because it leaked at the shoulder. The slightest trickle when Houdini first climbed into it would have been a giveaway of the secret, so Houdini's usual procedure was to enter the milk can as soon as it had been filled to shoulder level. He then made his "test dip," which caused so much water to pour from the top of the milk can and down over the sides, that any slight leakage would be simply regarded as an aftermath of the overflow.

Further filling of the can, more splashing, the last pouring just before the cover was locked on, all helped to hide that one trifling clue. At the finish, the water was well below shoulder level, since Houdini was no longer in the milk can, so there was then no chance that any leakage might show.

Another answer to the leakage problem was to construct a milk can with a joint so neatly fitted that no water could trickle through, but that raised other difficulties. For one thing, too tight a fit could cause the parts to jam too solidly, making it harder to escape; for another, repeated working of the contrivance and the jolts it took in travel would have loosened it anyway.

There was, of course, another way to render the milk can leak-proof, or, as Houdini styled it, "airtight." That was to eliminate the "break" at the shoulder and provide some other mode of escape.

The simplest and most efficient device was a sliding collar made to fit over the actual neck of the milk can and apparently solidly riveted to the slanted section just below. This "shell" collar was provided with staples to receive the hasps that extended downward from the cover of the milk can.

Once the curtains of the cabinet were closed, the performer had only to push up the false collar, carrying the padlocked cover with it, thus making his escape by coming up through the neck, the very route by which he entered the milk can at the outset.

With a well-constructed milk can, this double collar not only stood the closest inspection, but actually made the device look more than ordinarily formidable. Fitted with a secret catch to hold it firmly in place, the collar could be released by the performer during his first dip, so that it was in readiness for the escape to follow.

There were various reasons why the special collar was not used on the original milk can. As already stated, the escape was adapted from a cylindrical tank, so the "shoulder" was the logical point of vulnerability. Again, the neck may have looked too obvious at the start; only when the device had undergone the positive test of repeated presentation could improvements be introduced.

Houdini experimented with several types of milk cans, which were mentioned in his notes under such terms as the "Old Style Can" and the "1908 Can." Just when he may have used the "collar" type in preference to the "shoulder" style is an interesting question in itself.

On Friday, November 13, 1908, Houdini's act was witnessed at the Oxford Theatre in London, by Ellis Stanyon, one of the leading authorities on magic at that time. Stanyon wrote a detailed description of the Milk Can Escape, which included this explanation:

> The straight neck would admit of an extra round and continuous band being pressed over it, fitting somewhat tightly and being of the same depth as the neck itself. The upper edge of such band could be wired all round, which would provide a proper finish and moreover hide the juncture between it and the top of the neck proper; the lower and sharp edge of the band would be effectually concealed in the angle formed by the juncture of the neck ... The lid would be made with a flange to sit *inside* the neck of the can and would also be provided with six hasps rivetted to the top, hinged at the extreme edge of the lid and situated at equal distances all round the same so as to fall over the six staples on the loose band.

This has been quoted verbatim because of its speculative tone, as though it were suggesting how the escape could have been accomplished, rather than furnishing positive data. Stanyon modified this with the concluding statement: "The above is, of course, my own explanation, not necessarily the method employed by Houdini."

By that Stanyon covered himself, whether his guess was right or wrong. But it still leaves the question: How right or wrong was his explanation? Stanyon saw the milk can a year after its invention, when Houdini was presumably using the type that broke apart at the shoulder. This was to some extent confirmed by Houdini's own personal notes on various Milk Can Escapes, when they were made public after his death.

In that case, Stanyon's guess was wrong, but if so, he either hit on an idea that Houdini already had in mind, or he provided a suggestion that was workable in its own right, for the milk can with the sliding collar definitely came into vogue later. Yet Stanyon's description of such a device apparently stands as the first on record.

An interesting feature in this comparison of milk cans is the placement of the handles, which were used to lift the milk can and tilt it to pour out the water afterward. A photograph of an early Houdini milk can shows the handles located on the slant between the shoulder and the neck. In his notes on "improvements" for the milk can, Houdini called for the handles to be "down lower" so that no hand-cuffs could be hooked on to "keep the lid on."

In short, some "smart" committee men might use cuffs instead of padlocks on two of the staples, locking one end of each handcuff to a staple, the other to a handle of the milk can, which would definitely impede the operation of the sliding collar, thus preventing or hindering the escape.

This indicates that the "lid" included the sliding collar, which was why the handles should be placed below "shoulder" level, too far for a pair of cuffs to stretch. A photo-graph of the final milk can, from which Hardeen escaped almost forty years after the trick was originated, shows the handles down below. In forty years, the "gag" as Houdini termed the secret, was raised from "shoulder" to "neck." In that same period, the handles were dropped from "slant" to "body." As the interior and unseen mechanism went upward, the outside and visible evidence went downward and nobody was any wiser; nobody, except those already "in the know."

That, in a single word, was the "magic" of it. Tomorrow, another Houdini could borrow a forgotten milk can from yesterday and baffle today's men and women just as effectively as ever.

Ellis Stanyon, who published his comments in a monthly magazine that was appropriately called *Magic* was in one definite sense both more mistaken and prophetic than he realized. In his brief review of the show that he saw on Friday the 13th, he commented that on that evening, the milk can was filled with milk, as the result of a "challenge" arranged between Houdini and the Alliance Dairy Company, "the idea being, owing to the density of the milk, to render the escape more difficult, if not impossible."

That, of course, was merely part of the "promotion," a bit of press agentry that plugged the sponsor and at the

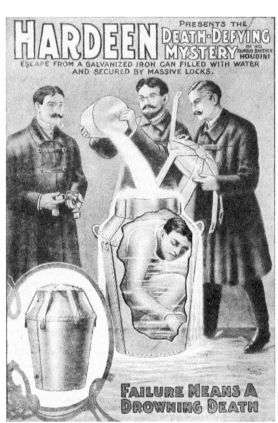

Fig. 30. *Poster advertising Hardeen's milk can act.*

same time provided a false lead of a sort, where the secret of the escape was concerned. In that regard, Stanyon added:

> I am of the opinion, however, that the density of the fluid and in which the performer is undoubtedly completely immersed for a period of time well under the minute, does not in any way effect the escape; for that matter, the churn might just as well be filled with Stout, but I understand Mr. Houdini is a teetotaler.

Years later Hardeen, who was also a teetotaler, worked the Milk Can Escape for a big distilling concern, using a much diluted mixture of whisky as the fluid. In that instance, the fluid had a decided effect on the escape, just as it would have in Houdini's case, had he used stout instead of milk. Alcoholic fumes formed and filled the air space so rapidly that Hardeen was almost knocked out before he started the escape and he was lucky to emerge alive.

One highly dramatic touch was provided in the Milk Can Escape as performed by both Houdini and Hardeen. As soon as the curtained front of the cabinet was closed, an assistant armed with a fire-ax took his stand there and peered through the corner of the curtain, looking into the cabinet from the outside.

This was by no means a mere theatrical touch, as Hardeen's experience with the milk can proves. There was always the chance that something might go wrong, either with the milk can or the escape artist himself. It was then the business of the man with the ax to come to the rescue, and quickly.

Houdini entrusted that task to his chief assistant, Collins, who continued with Hardeen after Houdini's death. The fact that an ax was a sufficiently powerful implement to effect a rescue within a mere minute or two, was in itself an indication that the milk can, although sturdy, was by no means as formidable a contrivance as it looked to be. This, however, did not occur to the average onlooker.

Naturally, the quickest emergency exit would be created by forcing it open at the neck or shoulder, according to the type of milk can being used, but the instructions called for Collins to chop a hole lower down on the side of the milk can so that the water would gush out. That would have saved Houdini from a "drowning death" which was advertised as the great peril that he faced in this escape.

There was one other type of milk can that figured heavily in Houdini's calculations. That was the unprepared milk can, a bona fide model that could be displayed in a theater lobby, given the most stringent examination, yet used in an escape, if need be.

While actually "unprepared," this type of milk can was at least of special design. It had only three sets of hasps and staples attached to the lid and collar respectively. In the case of the staples, copper rivets were used and just one to each staple. The rivet heads were on the inside, with felt washers between them and the neck of the can. The protruding ends were fitted with square bolts on the outside.

To effect his escape, Houdini had to smuggle in a small but strong pair of cutting pliers, in order to cut one of the rivets, thus loosening one staple. That enabled the lid of the can to hinge up on the other two hasps, allowing a prompt escape. The pliers were fitted with a tiny bag to catch the rivet head, rather than have it remain in the bottom of the milk can as a telltale clue.

Replacement of the rivet was accomplished by pushing a duplicate through from the inside and setting the loose staple over it, then bolting it in place. All this required rapid action, particularly in the early stages, where the danger lay. So Houdini's specifications called for a bulging "bell" top to allow him repeated breaths of air, in case the cutting of the rivet took longer than anticipated. Again, the ax man was on hand and watching in case it took too long.

Other Milk Can Escapes

ALMOST FROM THE TIME when Houdini introduced the Milk Can Escape, rival performers began explaining it, copying it, and even "inventing" it according to the stories that they gave. Within a few years the "Houdini Milk Can" was offered for sale by magical dealers both in America and abroad.

By then Houdini had moved on to other types of escapes, but he left a trail of milk cans—experimental and finished— and it is doubtful that anyone ever exactly duplicated the favorite milk cans used by Houdini and Hardeen. On the contrary, Houdini must have tested out or in some way improved almost every type of workable device in that general category. One of the earliest "explanations" offered was that of a milk can with a double lining, or more strictly speaking, a bottomless milk can sliding down into an outer shell, which was simply a cylinder with a solid bottom.

By pushing the inner can downward, its lower rim came flush with the bottom, while the band encircling the shoulder came over the upper rim of the outer shell. As with the Houdini milk can that broke at the shoulder, the double-lined type also required false rivet heads around the shoulder band. Since the inner lining was part of the can proper, it had a solid appearance, inside as well as outside.

The only trouble with this cleverly designed contrivance was that it would not work (or could be worked only with great difficulty) as originally described, because all the milk cans of that day had an outward slant, from bottom up to shoulder. The performer not only had to push the entire lining clear up and off, but it would tend to wobble when he did so.

Later the inner lining was adapted to a straight-walled style of milk can, where the "push" was directly upward. This was more practical, but still had certain disadvantages.

Within six months after Houdini first presented the Milk Can Escape, Will Goldston, a London magical author and dealer, published a book on *Tricks and Illusions* in which he described an "Escape from Milk Can Securely Padlocked."

According to Goldston, he had worked on an escape involving a zinc-lined barrel three years before and he "took it" that the Milk Can Escape had "emanated" from that idea.

Goldston's contraption looked more like a churn than a milk can, though it was made of metal, not wood, and had a flanged lid with staples that fitted through slots and could be locked by hanging padlocks on them. It could be filled with water clear up to the top so there was no chance of leakage, the escape hatch being located in the very top.

The trick consisted of a tight-fitted disk in the center of the lid. This was provided with a hidden hinge and could be sprung open with the aid of a thin steel blade that was smuggled into the milk can. Needless to say, Goldston's curious contrivance furnished no competition to Houdini's authentic-looking milk can but it did encourage other self-styled escape kings to question his priority and build milk cans resembling Houdini's own, outwardly at least.

One imitator, Clempert, put on an act with two identical milk cans, which was reviewed at an English provincial theater in June 1909, slightly more than six months after Houdini had first shown the Milk Can Escape in London. The review ran:

> A committee from the audience having inspected the cans, also the locks, Clempert's lady assistant is put into one of the cans without water, the lid is placed on and locked. The second can is then filled with apparently boiling water, the performer steps in, the lid is placed on and locked. A canopy is then moved forward over the cans, curtains drawn, while attendants with watches and hatchets take up their position outside.
>
> In about one and one-half minutes, the curtains are withdrawn and the performer comes forward, the cans appearing not to have been disturbed. But upon removing the locks and lid of the can containing the water, and in which the performer had been immersed, the lady is discovered therein; the other can being empty.

An analysis of this double mystery shows that actually only one special or "trick" milk can was necessary, the other being entirely unprepared. This gave the performer a decided "edge" over the committee, as he could steer any "tough" or overskeptical committee men to the unprepared milk can, keeping them busy examining it until they no longer had time to look over the "fixed" one.

The special milk can, of course, was the one that contained the water. It had to be worked rapidly in order to speed up the "quick change" and for that reason a milk can with a sliding collar was probably the best. Whether or not Clempert was familiar with that type is a question, but actually it is unimportant, as other styles would have filled the bill as well.

The procedure, however, was this: The girl was locked in the ordinary milk can, where she could stay comfortably for half an hour or more, as she was surrounded entirely by air, not water. But she didn't have to stay that long, not by any means. The performer, locked in the water-filled milk can, not only made a rapid escape, but proceeded to unlock the padlocks on the can that contained his assistant, using duplicate keys.

Once the girl was out, she helped the performer replace and lock the padlocks; then clambered into the trick milk can, which was promptly closed. The performer therewith emerged from the cabinet, took his bow, and had the committee open the water-filled milk can to produce the girl from it. After that, the ordinary milk can was opened and shown empty.

There was another interesting phase to this act: In most "trick" milk cans, a special interior catch could be used to prevent the can from "breaking" either at shoulder or neck, during the preliminary inspection. Such a catch could be quickly released by the performer, once he entered the milk can. But "setting" the catch after the escape was something that provided problems, since the performer was outside the milk can. With the two milk can acts performed by Clempert and his lady assistant, that difficulty was eliminated. While the performer was out front taking his bow, the girl was tightening the inside catches so that the trick milk can, once it was unlocked and its occupant removed, could be examined all over again without danger of detection.

Of course, now the girl was in a milk can that contained water, quite unlike the empty one that she had entered originally. But there was a lot less water because the performer, being bulkier, had displaced most of it. So the girl had plenty of air to breathe while she was racing to get the inside catches fixed before the assistants unlocked and removed the outside padlocks.

There was one other detail, the matter of the boiling water. Actually, it wasn't boiling, it was just quite hot. Assistants poured water from big kettles or containers that had just been brought to a boil at the top, but was still cool at the bottom, so that when the performer jumped into the milk can, he mixed it and reduced the temperature. That was an old Oriental trick that had become little more than a sideshow stunt but gave a dramatic touch to the dual milk can mystery.

By the time the girl entered the half-filled milk can the water was merely warm. So Clempert's lady assistant had little more to do than pose as a bathing beauty, which in that period, was almost the same as appearing in full dress.

But in reducing the temperature of the water, Clempert lowered that of the audience as well. From a fever-pitch of waiting while Houdini eluded a drowning death, audiences showed a lukewarm reaction to a quick-change act in which a pair of milk cans figured as mere props.

The professional as well as the public reaction to this cheapening of a truly sensational mystery was reflected in the following notes which appeared in the *Wizard*, a British magical magazine conducted by P. T. Selbit, at that same time:

Houdini has been doing great things in the way of sensational outdoor advertising during the past fortnight in Scotland. In the presence of enormous crowds he has been making manacled dives in the local harbors and channels, and creating enough discussion to ensure more than enough patrons to fill the accommodation of the theaters in which he has played.

If all magic acts put themselves to some inconvenience to draw the public outside of their actual performance on the stage, we should find a brisker demand for illusionists and a general rise in their salaries. But do not copy another artist's advertising schemes. There are more ways than one of letting people know you are worthwhile.

John Clempert is paying Houdini the compliment of imitating his act as closely as possible, plus the favor of an exposé of the latter's milk can mystery. Clempert is "the man they could not hang."[2] Perhaps this is a pity for when one man gets to work on another's reputation and has the impudence to rub the fact home by exposing the methods of the originator, words are useless.

When in Aberdeen a few days since, Houdini found the grave of John Henry Anderson, the Wizard of the North, in a neglected state and with characteristic thought, he had it put to rights and the gravestone repainted.

That may explain why Houdini is still remembered, whereas Clempert would be totally forgotten, except for

---

2 This referred to an act formerly performed by Clempert, in which he slipped free of a hangman's noose tied about his neck by a committee from the audience.

the record, such as this. How far Clempert went toward "exposing" the Milk Can, the writer in the *Wizard* did not specify. But Houdini continued to draw crowds when he presented the original mystery in his own inimitable way.

As to the mechanics of the Milk Can, two years later (in 1911) the Mysto Magic Company in New Haven, Connecticut, included "Houdini's Milk Can Escape" in its catalog, with the statement:

> The milk can which we offer for sale is worked on a principle decidedly different from the cheap imitations of this wonderful trick. In the first place, the milk can which we furnish will positively bear the most minute examination ...

> It can be filled with water if so desired and the performer placed in the center and securely locked in by padlocks and staples. As soon as the screen is placed in front of him, he makes an instantaneous escape. Everything bears examination before and after the trick.

547. **HOUDINI'S MILK CAN ESCAPE.**

Made famous by H. Houdini. The milk can which we offer for sale is worked on a principle decidedly different from the cheap imitations of this wonderful trick. In the first place the milk can which we furnish will positively bear the most minute examination. As usual, our guarantee stands back of our milk can. It can be filled with water if so desired, and the performer placed in the center, and securely locked in by padlocks and staples. As soon as the screen is placed in front of him, he makes an instantaneous escape. Everything bears examination before and after the trick.

Note.—The performer can be securely shackled if so desired, before being placed in the can. Price $35.00.

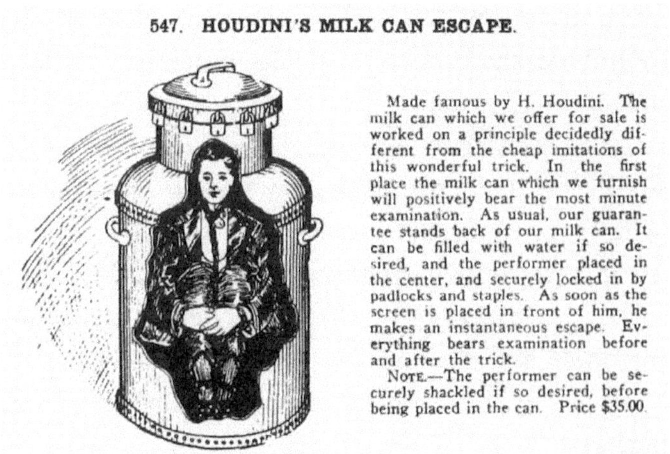

Fig. 31. *Advertisement in Mysto Magic catalog for trick milk can.*

The milk can illustrated with this description is of the straight-walled type, which could have worked in any of three ways, either at the shoulder, by means of a sliding neck, or as a double milk can with an inner lining. It was priced at $35.00, so perhaps the best way of solving the mystery would be to figure the manufacturing costs of that day.

After Hardeen's death, in 1945, the milk can that he used was advertised for $500 and sold for that price. In 1961 a manufacturer of magical equipment was offering the Famous Houdini Milk Can Escape for $550.

The straight-walled milk can with the double lining is usually equipped with a bayonet catch at the bottom, thus preventing it from coming loose during the preliminary examination.

The usual mode of release was to turn the lining in the right direction in order to free the catch; then push the lining straight upward, the outer wall of the milk can guiding its course.

There is no chance of leakage at the shoulder with this type of milk can as the interior is solid, clear to the top, and by having the outer can made watertight, there is no leakage at the bottom.

From this developed an even more ingenious version of the "double-walled" milk can in which the two parts were reversed. Here we find the outer shell to be the actual milk can, so that its entire surface, including shoulders, neck, and collar, can not only be thoroughly examined, but have nothing fake about them, not even in the form of false rivets, except at the very bottom, where trickery is least to be suspected.

The outer shell is bottomless and its lower edge slides down into a snug but ample space within a metal band which appears to be riveted there, but is actually part of the inner lining, which has a solid bottom. These rivets are generally false, but since the outer shell has slots to fit over hidden pins and form a bayonet catch, some of the rivets could go clear through and serve as pins as well.

In this improved type of milk can, the inner lining can be extended clear up to the collar if desired, concealing its upper edge more effectively than if it terminated at the shoulder. The performer must gain a grip inside the collar in order to turn it and the outer shell as well. One way of doing this is with a pronged tool that can be fitted into air holes in the cover and given a twist, thus turning the loose-fitting outer shell as well. A still better and safer plan is to release the catch before getting into the milk can or before putting on the lid. This can be done by the assistants while they are filling the milk can with water, or by the performer when he first dips into the milk can and then emerges. During that action he naturally places his hands on the upper rim and to supply the necessary twist is just a matter of course.

That one factor, safety, is the disadvantage with any milk can of the double-walled type. It isn't just a case of an escape artist risking his reputation with a "gaff" that fails to work; his life is literally at stake as well. This was fully evidenced in the case of Genesta, an escape artist who worked the milk can in theaters throughout the United States.

Always, the milk can was supposed to be tested prior to the act, but one night the show arrived late and was set up so hurriedly that this was overlooked. Genesta was locked in the milk can as usual and when he failed to escape within three or four minutes, his assistants realized that an emergency had arrived and they promptly became excited.

They pulled away the cabinet and frantically tried to unlock the half dozen padlocks that held the top in place, but the keys had become mixed and more minutes were lost in the confusion of finding the right ones. When the milk can was finally opened, Genesta was found drowned. The very ingenuity of the mechanism was the cause of this disaster. The milk can had been dropped while being loaded on a truck and its side had been dented just enough to lock the inner and outer walls, so the push-up wouldn't work.

With proper planning, such an emergency might have been met, but there is still a question whether a man with an ax could chop through a double wall in time. That is why the simpler milk can of a "break-away" type is probably preferable. Most press photos of Houdini and Hardeen show them working in a milk can with slanted sides, which signifies either a shoulder-lift or a neck-slide, rather than a double-walled device.

Escape from a Block of Ice

In this unusual escape the performer is imprisoned in a covered iron cylinder which is effectively closed from the top. A huge block of ice, hollowed in the center, is placed over the cylinder and comes down to the platform, which is raised from the stage. Hence the man inside must not only escape from the cylinder; he must also overcome the heavy cake of ice.

The cover that fits on the cylinder is not hinged; it is fitted with hasps that fit over staples on the cylinder, and it cannot be removed by any usual method after the cake of ice is in position.

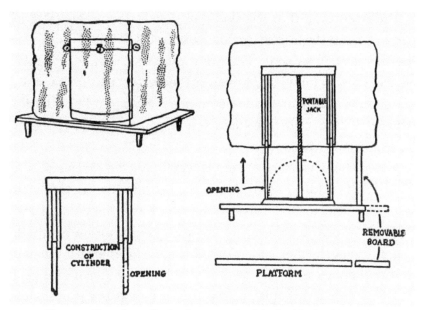

Fig. 32. *How the cylinder is covered with the block of ice; also construction of the cylinder and details of the escape.*

The secret of this escape lies in the construction of the cylinder, which has very thick walls and will stand a close inspection. The thick wall is really three layers of metal. First a thin cylinder with a solid bottom is constructed, and a hole is cut in the side above the bottom. The hole is large enough for a person to pass through. Then a double cylinder or shell is made; it has no bottom, and its walls are several inches apart, being closed at the top. This fits over the original cylinder, and when it is in position it hides the secret opening both inside and outside. By lifting this shell, the opening is revealed and the performer can make use of it. If desired, short bolts may pass through the inner wall of the shell into the genuine cylinder and thus prevent anyone from lifting the shell; if a tight fit of shell and cylinder is obtained, this is hardly necessary.

But assuming that the bolts are used, their removal and replacement from the inside will free the shell, and the performer can raise it. The great difficulty then is the cake of ice. It is so heavy that even if the performer can raise it, he cannot hold it up while he makes his escape. That is why the ice is used: to direct suspicion away from the true secret of the iron cylinder.

When the performer enters the cylinder, he carries a jack concealed on his person. Inside the cylinder he fits this jack together and uses it to raise the shell and the cake of ice. The sides of the cake of ice make it really an outer shell. Then the performer comes out through the opening. He can lower the jack from below, but this has two disadvantages; it is not only a difficult process, but it leaves the jack inside the cylinder at the finish. To overcome this the ends of the platform are used. They are removable, and the performer places them so that they will hold up the outer shell and the cake of ice. Having made his escape, he puts the end boards of the platform in position, drops the jack and removes it, and then knocks the boards out of the way so that the shell and the cake of ice come down to the platform. The ends of the platform are replaced, the jack is concealed, and every-thing is ready for the committee. When the jack is raised it presses against the inside of the cover, which is attached to the outer part of the shell. The center cylinder does not need to extend clear to the top of the shell; hence the staples for the locks can be bolted or riveted all the way through. It is advisable to have an air hole in the center of the cover, with a corresponding hole in the center of the cake of ice, as the escape is not a rapid one and the performer will need air.

The Mailbag Escape

THIS HAS SOMETIMES been classed as Houdini's greatest escape and from the standpoint of ingenuity, it has some claim to that title. But there was another factor that makes the Mailbag Escape worthy of a top rating: Houdini's claim—more or less—that he could escape from anything. Safes, vaults, and other formidable contrivances had certain limitations; people couldn't bring them around to the theater and challenge him to get out of them like handcuffs.

They could bring a straitjacket, so Houdini was quick to figure how to work out of that. But there was one item that was even more common, to be found in every hamlet throughout America; the U.S. mailbag, big enough to contain a person, made of strongly stitched canvas and leather, with a strap passing through hasps so close together that it would be impossible to work a hand between them.

That strap was locked at the end by a padlock that positively could not be reached by anyone within the almost airtight bag.

Unless Houdini could find a way out of such a restraint, he might just as well give up the escape business. How long he may have known that before he thought of a way out, he never stated, but he was ready for the mailbag by the time he was first challenged to escape from one.

From then on, Houdini invited such challenges. Here is how one read when he was playing vaudeville at the Orpheum Theater in Los Angeles:

> Houdini will be locked into a leather mail pouch by post office officials. This pouch will be secured with the patent Rotary Government Mail Locks used on registered mail pouches. These locks are made by the government for the sole use of the Post Office Department.
>
> They are never allowed out of the possession of postal officials and their possession or use by others is an offense punishable by fine or imprisonment. The keys are never allowed to leave the post office and should Houdini fail to release himself he must be taken to the central post office to have the lock opened.

This escape was very cleverly advertised and publicized, because the one thing that Houdini did require was a key to the lock. It didn't matter whether he obtained the original, by temporarily switching a dummy key for it, or whether he acquired a duplicate, or had one made. He couldn't get out of the locked mailbag without it except by slashing the bag open or ripping it apart. But Houdini made his mailbag escapes in letter-perfect style. When he emerged from his cabinet, the mailbag was intact, and in the same mint condition as an unused postage stamp in a collector's album.

Yet what good was a key to anyone inside the bag, since it was impossible to reach out and use it?

The answer was one of Houdini's best secrets. It was the reason why he mentioned in his notes that the "Mailbag Escape" was the "greatest test possible in the United States of America." How he used the key *outside* the bag while he was *inside* was perhaps the neatest trick that Houdini ever did.

Houdini smuggled the key into the mailbag with him, which was easy, as the key was small and could be easily hidden. But with the key, he also smuggled a string, which was attached to it. It was a long string, and Houdini's first action was to wrap the other end around a button or otherwise affix it to his clothing, as the one thing he could not afford was to lose the key.

Though Houdini could not work his hand out through the narrow space between the upper edge of the bag and the

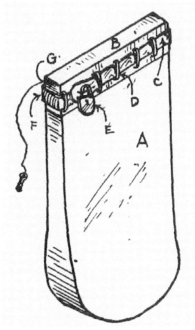

Fig. 33. *Mail bag construction. Locked bag with key on string.*

flap, he could push the key out. That is exactly what he did, paying out the string slowly and leaning the other way, so that the key would finally reach a fold in the canvas.

Probing the folds, Houdini found the key; then, by working his hand within the canvas, he gripped the lock.

It was almost like a puzzle, which through long practice, steady patience, and, above all, iron nerves could be accom-

Fig. 34. *Bag opened, strap released.*

plished with quick precision but that was just the beginning of Houdini's task.

The next job was like performing a delicate operation while wearing a pair of canvas mittens. Houdini had to unlock the padlock with the key, much like a game of blindman's buff, for he was working from the stifling pitch darkness within the bag, while the key was on the outside.

One false twist, one trifling slip and the key would be gone; not from clumsiness, but because quick twists and rapid moves were necessary to get to the desired goal. When the mishap occurred, the tied end of the string proved its value. By finding it, Houdini could haul in the key and start all over.

That happened very, very seldom; never twice during the same attempted escape, though Houdini still would have gone on, regardless of temporary setbacks. But always he finally found the keyhole and unlocked the padlock, which he then shook clear of the hasp and opened the bag, from which he emerged. The closing of the bag and the replacement of the lock followed; then Houdini appeared from the cabinet and took his bow, mailbag and all.

Another form of "Mailbag Escape" was introduced later. In this, a bar is put through holes in the top of a bag resembling a mailsack; and padlocks are put in holes on the ends of the bar to keep it closed. From this, the performer effects a quick release.

The trick depends on a special bar that unscrews in two sections; this bar is so perfectly made that it is impossible to find the joint. The padlocks furnish the leverage that makes it possible to "break" the bar swiftly and effectively.

It is a good trick, but it isn't the Houdini "Mailbag Escape." Nobody, apparently, has done it Houdini's way since Houdini himself performed it.

Walking Through A Brick Wall

IN THE SPRING of 1914 Houdini was completing a vaudeville tour through Scotland and England, featuring his upside-down "Water Torture Cell" escape and making plans for the coming season. In two successive years he had head-lined the summer bill at Hammerstein's Roof in New York, changing his program week by week, and he was scheduled to appear there again on the same basis.

During his British tour, Houdini had been carrying along various tricks and illusions for special "all-magical" programs that he occasionally presented in the provinces. It was his big ambition—which he was to achieve ten years later—to present a full evening of magic on the legitimate stage. This was a step in that direction, so Houdini was ready to buy or build any new illusion that intrigued him.

To find some such mystery that would also be sensa-tional enough to fill the bill at Hammerstein's was diffi-cult indeed, so Houdini was in luck when he met Sidney Josolyne, a London magician who was doing an Oriental act. Josolyne had been working on an idea of the very sort that Houdini wanted and was willing to let Houdini have it on very reasonable terms.

On May 4, 1914, at the New Cross Empire Theatre, Josolyne signed an agreement which gave Houdini the right to perform a mystery of walking through a steel wall, which Josolyne claimed as his origination.

That transaction apparently was as closely guarded as the secret of the mystery itself, for about the only inkling of it appeared in the May 1914 issue of the *Magician Monthly* in a brief sketch of Sidney Josolyne, wherein the writer stated:

Mr. Josolyne has confessed to us an undying devotion to magic and is everlastingly puzzling out new tricks and illusions...He also tells us that he has invented one illusion which he believes will puzzle every living magician and we are exceedingly anxious to see this ...

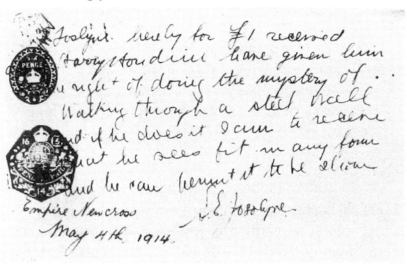

Fig. 35. *Josolyne's bill of sale for "Walking Through the Wall" trick. Sold to Houdini May 4, 1914.*

Undoubtedly that referred to the "Walking Through a Wall" which Josolyne must then have regarded as his greatest idea. Whether he had already sold it to Houdini is a question, but in all likelihood Josolyne made that statement after the transaction at the New Cross Empire. For one thing, the magazine may not have gone to press until about the middle of the month; for another, Josolyne's reticence even to hint at the nature of the illusion indicated that something was afoot; finally, if a question as to the invention came up later, the magazine item might help to substantiate Josolyne's claim.

Magical inventors considered it good policy to be ambiguous in their descriptions of their latest creations, often leaving much to the imagination. In the same issue of the *Magician Monthly,* reference was made to another genius in a paragraph which read:

> P. T. Selbit is about to "present" an entirely new and original wonder which at the moment he entitles "The Dissolving Man." In this instance, magicians will observe how surely science is being made to serve its purpose as an essential part of the magic art, and the manner in which the final effect is built up from the opening should be an object lesson to every magical showman.

Any link between Josolyne's unnamed masterpiece and Selbit's forthcoming attraction seemed very remote indeed; and there was no mention of Houdini in that issue. However, in the June number of the *Magician Monthly* we find these comments:

> Houdini concluded his stay in Great Britain with his last week's performance at the Nottingham Empire. June 18th will find him once more a passenger to America by the "Imperator." He opens

at Hammerstein's Roof Garden, New York City, July 6th, 1914. His act has developed of late into an illusion show and his program will contain much that is new and original with him. Houdini has many bookings before him which will make his absence from England a somewhat lengthy one.

In covering the English scene itself, the June issue of the *Magician Monthly* carried this comment:

> It is a pleasure also to note amongst the St. George's Hall arrangements, the appearance of Selbit in a new illusion in which he causes a man to walk through a brick wall!

St. George's Hall was an intimate theater that put on a complete bill of magical acts, under the auspices of the noted magical producers, Maskelyne and Devant. While the June *Magician Monthly* was going to press and Houdini was on his way to America, the London correspondent of the *Sphinx,* an American magical magazine, was penning these lines:

> At a private interview with Houdini, he informed me that on June 18th he sails for America, when he will open at Hammerstein's Roof Garden, New York, on July 6th, with the biggest illusion act in vaudeville. All the illusions are of his own invention, so one can expect a great show. Houdini is booked in America and abroad for a number of years, so it will be some little time before we shall have the opportunity of again witnessing his great act.

In the same "London Letter" the correspondent also announced:

> P. T. Selbit has just invented another new illusion called "Walking Through a Wall." This was exhibited at a private performance at Maskelyne and Devant's last Tuesday, with the result that it is booked right up into next March. Selbit opens with his latest mystery Monday, June 22nd, at the Hippodrome, Liverpool.

Another correspondent augmented that account with a brief review of Selbit's production. A girl—not a man—was the person who "dissolved" sufficiently to filter through the wall at the wizard's command.

Fig. 36. *"Walking Through the Wall" as sketched at St. George's Hall, London.*

Following the review, these comments were appended:

I understand Houdini has purchased the American rights for "The Wall Mystery" and intends to introduce this item in his Magical Revue at Hammerstein's, New York, on July 6th.

It would not astonish me if half a dozen people were not claiming to be the inventors of this illusion. I for one would be glad to know the name of the rightful owner, although Selbit, I think, has the full claim to the title.

By the time this appeared in print, in the *Sphinx* of July 1914, Houdini had already presented "Walking Through a Brick Wall" at Hammerstein's. He opened his first week with his already famous and highly popular Water Torture Cell and the Brick Wall was featured for the "second big week" commencing on July 13.

The advertisement in the *Sunday World* for July 12, 1914, ran as follows:

Houdini will walk through a Brick Wall. Despite a Vigilance Committee from audience. Houdini challenges any Bricklayer in the world to prove that the wall is prepared and defies the Bricklayers' Union to build a wall that he cannot penetrate under his conditions.

The general effect of the illusion, its style of presentation, and its impact on audience and public can best be gained from this firsthand description, which appeared in the *World Magazine* for August 2, 1914, exactly three weeks after the attraction was advertised:

WALKS THROUGH A BRICK WALL AND
MYSTIFIES MAGICIANS

Watch closely now, you clever ones. Here is a trick in magic which it will need all your cleverness to detect. It was recently shown in New York and is about the trickiest trick that has ever tricked a New York audience.

Not much paraphernalia here—just a big, brick wall built across the stage from back to front so that the audience can see both sides.

A man is going to "walk through the wall" without displacing a single brick. Look sharp!

Can you examine the wall? Certainly you can. You can also examine the floor. You needn't stay out there in the auditorium. Go up on the stage. Form a half-circle of clever ones behind the wall and on both sides, while the audience strains its eyes in front.

You can't find any trap doors. If there were any, they wouldn't do any good; the floor is covered with two large cloths, each a single piece. A man can't very well go through them without leaving a hole.

If he gets to the other side of the wall he won't do it by going down. Neither will he go up. The wall is just nine feet high and everybody can see over the top. And there isn't much chance of going around either end with the audience sitting in front and you standing in back.

Enter Harry Houdini, the "Handcuff King," the "Elusive American" they call him abroad. He stands solemnly beside the wall like a prisoner awaiting execution.

A little screen is placed around him. It is only six feet high and takes up not more than a third of the wall space. Another screen of the same size is placed on the other side of the wall.

Houdini's hands wave above the screen. "Here I am!" he cries. "Now I'm gone!"

Immediately, the screen which covered Houdini is taken away.

The prisoner is not there.

Immediately, the screen on the opposite side of the wall is taken away. There stands Houdini smiling serenely at the mystification of the clever ones.

Baffled, you say? Well, don't feel bad about it. This latest trick of Houdini has baffled every known expert in sleight-of-hand investigation. Among the spectators who have watched Houdini from the rear of Hammerstein's stage, where he has been doing this trick twice a day for two weeks, have been some of the greatest sleuths in magicdom in the United States. They all admit that they are baffled.

Just how was it accomplished? In order to make sure, this magazine asked Dr. Saram R. Ellison, an officer of the Magicians' Society, to inspect the working of the trick from the stage. Dr. Ellison has made a specialty of exposing the famous tricks of Herrmann the Great, Kellar, Thurston and Houdini.

"I'm puzzled," said Dr. Ellison. "In course of time we will discover how he does it, but at present it is beyond me. Several magicians who have seen the trick are equally at sea. It is obvious that Houdini does not go over the wall. Consequently, he must go through or under it. But I am certain that he does not employ trapdoors in the floor of the stage. I am able to do Houdini's Milk Can trick, but at the present time, the only man in the world who knows the secret of the brick wall trick is Houdini himself."

That it is a trick, is admitted. Houdini isn't supernatural and doesn't claim that it is anything but a trick. It is what might be called a "trick with a hole in it"; but so far, no one but Houdini has been able to find the hole. the wall has been examined by members of the audience at every performance and not a brick has been found misplaced.

The wall is not a trick. It is built on the stage twice a day with actual brick and mortar. Once a committee from Bricklayers' Union Number 34 was invited to build the wall. the trick was performed as usual. Not a brick had been moved so that anyone could notice it and the floor covering was apparently undisturbed.

Yes, this trick is distinctly Houdini's secret. He works it all alone. Even his "assistants" are spies, for the committee which places the screens against the wall and takes them away is selected from the audience.

Houdini isn't saying that the trick will never be detected. He is just doing the trick and letting the public guess. He wants to be watched. Being watched has been his chief enjoyment from the time he first bewildered country constables by slipping out of their handcuffs more quickly than they could slip them on. There is only one thing which he possibly enjoys more, and that is watching the faces of his audience when he has accomplished his trick. And he finds but little difference in facial expressions, whether the onlookers be country constables or blasé denizens of Broadway. On this, as on other occasions, they prove themselves brothers "under their skins." And when they show their amazement at discovering Houdini on the side of the wall where they all knew he was going to be, there is one face in the theatre which seems to show more enjoyment than any other. That is Houdini's.

In contrast to this highly graphic and detailed description of Houdini's New York presentation, the following terse review appeared in the British monthly, the *Magic Wand,* in regard to the Selbit performance:

> Presented by the inventor, Mr. P. T. Selbit, at a special performance held at St. George's Hall, on June 16th, the new illusion "Walking Through a Wall" bids fair to crowd England's Home of Mystery for some time to come.
>
> A large sheet of woven material, which is proved to be made of one piece, having been placed on the stage, members of the audience are invited to come up and inspect a real brick wall, which, having been erected on a steel girder, is placed in the center of the stage. With the aid of a hammer, the solidity of the wall is clearly demonstrated, a young lady is introduced, and a screen placed around her.
>
> The assistant is thus concealed from view, while a similar screen is placed in position on the other side of the wall. When screen number two is removed, the lady is discovered on the other side. The committee from the audience entirely surround the scene of this remarkable transportation.

A comparison of the two accounts shows that the illusion was obviously the same; but in America the public regarded it as Houdini's, while in England it was accepted as Selbit's. Another difference was that Houdini performed the mystery personally, by going through the Wall himself;

whereas Selbit simply showed it as a stage presentation, causing his lady assistant to pass through.

Of the two, Houdini's procedure was far stronger and more effective, as witness the publicity it brought from a single showing at Hammerstein's, while Selbit was making the round of the English music halls, which were always willing to welcome a novel act. But this mystery which the public classed as sensational, was fast becoming controversial in magical circles.

In the " London Letter" that appeared in the August 1914 *Sphinx,* the correspondent began with a glowing account of Walking Through a Wall which he defined as "the sole invention of Mr. P. T. Selbit" and then commented later:

> There has been considerable trouble in Bradford over the "new illusion" which I have written about in the beginning of my letter.
>
> It appears that another person has claimed to be the originator of "Walking Through a Wall," this being Mr. Josolyne, and it seems that Mr. Selbit put on a private performance for booking managers on June 2nd, while Mr. Josolyne sold the American rights to Harry Houdini on May 4th and deposited his plans of the invention with "The Performer" on June 15th. Mr. Selbit's act was booked to open at the Alhambra on Monday last, but on Thursday, the Moss Empire management put Mr. Josolyne's illusion into the program at the Empire. I do not think that the last has been heard of the above affair, but obviously both Mr. P. T. Selbit and Mr. Josolyne think themselves to be the inventor.

Whichever had claim to the illusion in England—Josolyne or Selbit—the fact remained that Houdini had obtained performing rights to Walking Through a Wall before either of the disputants had publicly presented the new sensation and had certainly established his American rights to the illusion.

But while the "war" between Selbit and Josolyne was dwindling to a tempest in a teapot in England where World War I had just begun and was fully gripping the public mind, Houdini was having trouble on the home front. In the September issue of the *Sphinx,* a New York magical dealer advertised the full secret for building and working, "Walking Through a Solid Brick, Wall" complete with blueprints, for the modest sum of $1.00.

The editor of the *Sphinx,* Dr. A. M. Wilson, had long been at odds with Houdini. Some years later they were to become the best of friends, but in the issue of October 1914, Dr. Wilson justified his running of the dollar ad by saying that it was all the advertiser claimed for it and that it was "worth the dollar, if only to satisfy curiosity as to how it is done."

Dr. Wilson then went on to state editorially:

> I dislike airing grievances or arousing controversy in the *Sphinx,* but in justice to the Great Alexander— now playing in California—I will have to state that he used the illusion of "Walking Through a Brick Wall" in his act as far back as December 1898 in the Palace Grand Theatre, in Dawson City, Alaska, using blocks of ice twelve inches thick instead of bricks; in Portland, Oregon, 1900, he used hollow tile; in the Cincograph Theatre, in San Francisco, using poured concrete.

Alexander has also used boiler iron, heavy planks as well as bricks. I had his plans and descriptions of the act for some time; they are almost identical with the description and model sent me by Dr. Saram R. Ellison of New York City. Dr. Ellison's model is complete in every detail, as are Alexander's drawings.

Assuming Alexander's claim to have been valid, it is very possible that reports of his Walking Through a Wall, performed in the early days of Pacific Coast vaudeville, could have reached England during the intervening years and there been improved, adapted, or reinvented into a new illusion .

Such things were common in magical circles, in fact still are. One performer will come up with a new idea or turn an old method into a different effect. Whenever the final version became a rousing success, it was customary for the person who performed the trick in its crude or primitive form to take credit for the completed concept.

The "model" mentioned in the *Sphinx* editorial raises an interesting point. Dr. Ellison, who had expressed himself as "amazed" when he witnessed Houdini's Walking Through a Wall at Hammerstein's, was an ardent collector of magical books who had acquired the largest magical library then extant, with the possible exception of Houdini's own.

Dr. Ellison had also fashioned models of illusions performed by leading magicians and had revealed their workings to the public through an earlier article in the New York *World;* but that was before Walking Through a Brick Wall had been invented or revived. So Dr. Ellison may still have been trying to ferret out the secret when he joined the committee on Houdini's stage in July 1914. By October, Dr.

Ellison had gained the answer, for he had a working model of the "Wall" in his collection.

Possibly the model had been built from the blueprint advertised in the September *Sphinx,* but it is more likely that it was obtained from another source. It might have been guessed by persons who repeatedly watched Houdini's show, for they could have narrowed down the possibilities.

Again, some backstage "bribery" may have figured; not where Houdini's own assistants were concerned, for they were not only loyal but sworn to secrecy where his methods were concerned; but in involving persons working around the theater.

Still more likely, the word may have leaked from England, where Selbit was presenting Walking Through a Wall at various vaudeville houses and another magician was showing it at St. George's Hall. With the feud between Josolyne and Selbit, magicians and public alike were curious about the mystery and, as with every magical controversy, the secret was due to pop out in order to support one performer's claim against the other. None of this pleased or helped Houdini. He preferred to feature one of his own originalities rather than the novelty which he had acquired as an exclusive—which it hadn't proved to be. So he dropped Walking Through the Wall and toured the Keith Circuit with the Water Torture Cell, which until then had never been seen off Broadway.

There were other reasons, however, why Houdini discarded the Wall illusion; these will become plain after studying the simple but ingenious secret of the mystery.

Analyzed, the feat of Walking Through a Wall offered the following possible solutions:

One was for the performer to go through the wall, which was utterly impossible when it was openly built of solid bricks; and therefore the first way to be rejected.

The next was for Houdini to go over the wall. which was preposterous, since it was 9 feet high, with a space of three feet between the top of the screens and the top of the wall.

Another way was to go around it, which seemed equally unlikely, as it was farther around the wall than over it; and the wall was surrounded by a committee, as well as in full view of the audience.

That left only one way—under the wall. But that was the first way to be ruled out, for the reason that it was impossible for Houdini to go down through a trap door on one side of the wall and come up through a trap on the other, because of the seamless cloth that was first spread on the stage to prove that traps were not used.

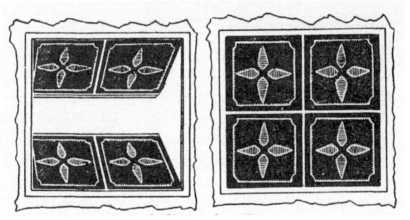

Fig. 37. *Center pattern of rug opened and closed.*

In fact, traps were *not* used, because only one trap was required. This single trap was long enough to include the space within both screens and thickness of the wall between

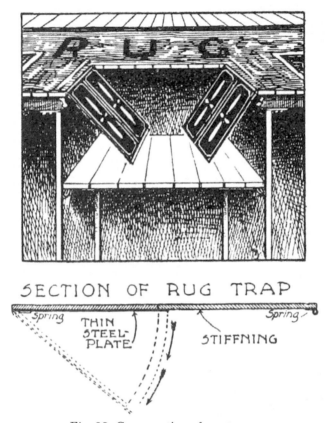

SECTION OF RUG TRAP

Spring   THIN STEEL PLATE   STIFFNING   Spring

Fig. 38. *Cross section of rug trap.*

them. The fact that the trap was covered with the cloth made it all the easier for Houdini to work his way beneath the wall once the trap was lowered from below stage, because the cloth supported him as it sagged beneath his weight.

Once Houdini was under and up on the other side, the trap was closed from below and the stage was as solid as ever. The cloth, too, was intact, and by laying it loosely at the outset, any slack resulting from the sag would remain unnoticed at the finish.

Actually, two cloths were essential to the trick. One had to be on the stage at the start, otherwise, the committee men would have noticed the trap door. So the first cloth was a large one, serving as a carpet. It was the smaller cloth that was shown to be seamless, fully examined, and spread exactly where the wall and screens were to go.

While both cloths could sag beneath the performer, that was not the preferred method. Houdini's full specifications called for the large cloth to be an actual carpet, with a special pattern, so that it could be cut to fit the trap door. Such "rug traps" had been used in other illusions and the cut could not be noticed at a distance of more than a few feet.

The trap was hinged in two sections, dropping downward at the center. When lowered, they formed a V-shaped trough just deep enough for the performer to wiggle through, yet they would "give" a little more, as needed.

This minimized the sag in the cloth and supported most of the performer's weight during the passage beneath the wall.

When a large rug or carpet was used, the committee could stand on it while the illusion was in progress. There would be no sagging or stretching of the rug because of its cut-out center. Only the smaller cloth would dip into the trap.

Once hidden by the first screen, Houdini gave a signal; the trap was lowered and he made his way beneath the wall; once up on the other side, he signaled for the closing of the trap and emerged from the second screen. All the while, thousands of eyes were watching the screens, the top of the wall, and practically counting the bricks from end to end; checking every possible route except the one that Houdini actually took!

Stage traps had been used with many illusions and various measures had been taken to disguise them. Alexander could have presented Walking Through a Wall according to his claim, using the trap door method, yet without the added feature of the special covering that allowed the committee to surround the wall and apparently made use of a trap door impossible. That was the selling point of the Josolyne version, as acquired by Houdini.

Now for the real reasons why Houdini did not go on with the Walking Through a Wall as he easily could have, after the mild furor had passed. First and most important, his own situation had changed completely. When Houdini left England in June 1914, he definitely announced plans for a full evening show; in fact, had been working toward that end and had purchased rights to Walking Through a Wall as one of the features. Now a big show was no small order, particularly as it meant competing with Thurston, who had a strong hold on that field.

Houdini always had an "out" for everything, and he needed one in this case, as he couldn't afford to risk his reputation in a losing cause. His "out" happened to be the European bookings that he had also mentioned. In short, if Houdini had found the change-over from a vaudeville headliner to a star in a legitimate show would take too long to pay off, he could have cut short his American tour and gone to Europe to recoup his losses.

The sudden outbreak of World War I canceled all possible European engagements, but fortunately for Houdini, it came before he had invaded the legitimate field. How long the war would last was debatable, so meanwhile Houdini took an American vaudeville tour, as stated.

But all his advance publicity on Walking Through a Brick Wall went to naught.

The illusion could have been used on the stage of any legitimate theater, because all were fitted with traps and others could be cut as needed. In Thurston's show, perhaps 50 per cent of the illusions depended on traps and Houdini could have used them too, particularly in Walking Through a Brick Wall.

But traps were practically taboo in many of the better vaudeville palaces. No magicians appearing in such theaters used traps; at least not as a rule. Having one cut to size in the exact center of the stage—as was necessary with the Wall illusion—would have been unthinkable. Mr. Albee, the genteel overlord of the Keith Circuit, wouldn't have allowed it with his nice new stages.

No trap, no brick wall; so that was the end of it. But there was another reason, too. During his engagement at Hammerstein's, where he had the trap facilities, Houdini recognized that Walking Through a Brick Wall was too slow for an American vaudeville audience. It was all build-up; then the thing was done, with no danger, no suspense, as in the Water Torture Cell.

It also lacked general audience appeal, as only the persons near the center aisle could see both sides of the brick wall and thus view both screens at the same time. They witnessed the illusion before and after—but people at one side saw only that Houdini was gone from the first screen; while those at the other side saw him come from the second screen.

What went on over on the other side, they didn't know; and in America, that meant they wouldn't care. In England, such "problem" illusions were something of a rage and spectators were quite happy to know that somebody else was witnessing what went on, even if they didn't. But not in America.

Somehow, the notion got about that Houdini abandoned Walking Through a Brick Wall because the local stagehands could learn how the trick was done and spread the news about town.

If that had bothered Houdini, he wouldn't have bought the illusion in the first place. He knew all about stagehands and their garrulous ways, having been in the business a lot longer than anyone who might have come up with that idea.

Houdini had an alternate way of presenting Walking Through a Brick Wall without the use of a trap at all. It has been claimed that he worked it during his New York engagement; and while this is doubtful, he may have introduced it at certain performances. Certainly it would have been in keeping with his policy of varying his methods. What was more, if he had gone on the road with a big show—as he then intended—he could have switched to the alternate routine in theaters where the act was billed, but a suitable trap proved unavailable. Anyone who knew Houdini will agree that he would never have let such circumstances catch him without something in reserve.

The alternate method was not to go under the wall—which was impossible without a trap—but to go around it, which still was feasible, even though going over the wall or through it were totally out of the question. But how could Houdini go around the wall from one screen to the other, with a few thousand people looking on?

The answer was that the bricklayers, workmen, and Houdini's assistants were wearing smocks while they completed the building of the wall and put the screens in place. In the folds of the first screen was a duplicate smock. When the screen was placed about Houdini, he slid the smock over his shoulders and stepped out past the end panel of the threefold screen, toward the far end of the wall.

The other panels hid this action from the front, and smocked assistants masked Houdini's getaway at the back as they adjusted the screen in place. Disguised as another workman, Houdini went around the wall and helped put the second screen on the other side. Again hidden by a small cluster of arriving helpers, he stepped into the screen from in back and it was closed around him .

There Houdini peeled off the smock and was again in evening clothes, as at the outset of the process. After he made his appearance from the second screen, it was folded and taken away with the smock inside it.

The specifications for this method also called for a pair of dummy hands, fitted into the first screen, which would appear and wave above the screen, actuated by a cord handled by an assistant. This was to convey the impression that Houdini was inside that screen up until the last moment.

Such a device was not entirely necessary, as in actuality Houdini could have gone around the rear end of the wall and reached the other screen just as rapidly as by crawling under the wall via the trap door route.

The feasibility of this method is unquestioned, as the "disguised assistant" routine has been used successfully in various "quick change" acts. It allows for added features, such as placing a sheet of glass or metal on the stage to prove the absence of any traps.

But the trap door device still stands as the basic method, as is witnessed by the fact that at St. George's Hall in London, a lady penetrated the brick wall without the presence on the stage of committee women or lady bricklayers.

The Vanishing Elephant

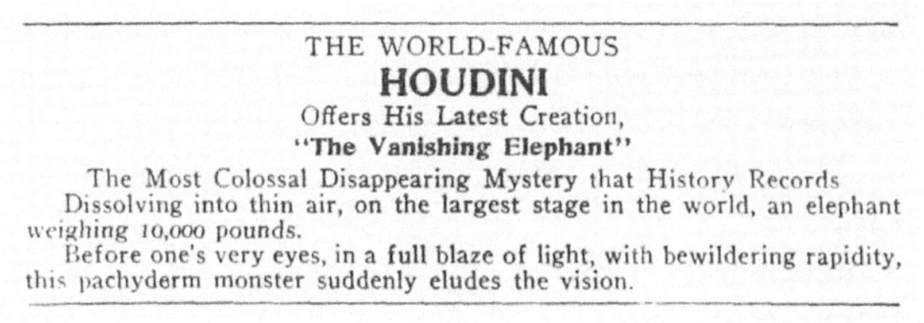
THE WORLD-FAMOUS

HOUDINI

Offers His Latest Creation,

"The Vanishing Elephant"

The Most Colossal Disappearing Mystery that History Records

Dissolving into thin air, on the largest stage in the world, an elephant weighing 10,000 pounds.

Before one's very eyes, in a full blaze of light, with bewildering rapidity, this pachyderm monster suddenly eludes the vision.

Fig. 39

PERHAPS THE "BIGGEST" ILLUSION ever performed was Houdini's "Vanishing Elephant," which he introduced on January 7, 1918 at the famous New York Hippodrome, where it was appropriately presented on what was then regarded as the world's largest stage.

That in itself tells why the "life" of the illusion was limited practically to that one engagement, which continued through the next few months. The Hippodrome at that time featured a troupe of trained elephants, so the illusion was literally "built around" one of the performing pachyderms.

The specification naturally called for a huge cabinet, which was all the better from the Hippodrome's standpoint because the mammoth stage would have dwarfed the average illusion. The stronger and more solid the construction, the better it could stand the elephant's tonnage. So the illusion was not designed to "travel" like most magical equipment; and even if it had been, the whole setup—elephant, cabinet, and all—would have been too large in proportion to many of the stages that Houdini would have encountered on tour.

As a sample of the Hippodrome's immensity, one of the spectacles presented there was the setting up of an actual circus tent, minus the side walls, so that the theater audience could witness an abbreviated circus performance "under canvas," which in turn was watched by a "stage audience" gathered about the arena. It was in this "circus ring" that the entire troupe of elephants appeared as the feature act.

Contemporary accounts of the Vanishing Elephant are comparatively few, as it was simply billed as part of the Hippodrome's extravaganza and World War I was raging in full intensity, capturing most of the nation's headlines. If Houdini had toured with the trick, it would have undoubtedly commanded detailed reviews and created local discussion among magicians in many cities. As it stands, such reports are sparse indeed.

The best, and to a great extent the fairest, description of the illusion was that supplied by Houdini himself to the magician magazine, the *Sphinx,* where it appeared in March 1918, while Houdini was still presenting the mystery. Houdini's statement ran:

I have been prolonged at the Hippodrome as the Vanishing Elephant is creating so much talk and really it is the biggest vanish the world has ever seen. I have a wonderful elephant and it is stated that she is the daughter of the famous Jumbo.

I use a cabinet about eight feet square, about twenty-six inches off the floor; it is rolled on by twelve men. I show all parts, opening back and front. The elephant walks into it; I close the doors and curtains—doors in the back and curtains in the front— and in two seconds I open back and front and she is gone.

No special background, in full glare of the lights, and it is a weird trick. In fact, everyone says, "We don't see enough of it." They are so busy watching for false moves that though the trick takes seven or eight minutes, it appears like a few seconds.

Houdini went on to relate some highlights of his presentation, which are very interesting as a personalized account. He commented:

The elephant salutes me, says goodbye to the audience by waving her trunk and head, turns to me, lifts up her trunk as if to give me a kiss. In fact, I say to the audience, "Jennie will now give me a kiss" but she is really coming to me with her mouth open for sugar, with which I trained her. I introduce her as the first known Vanishing Elephant.

She has a baby blue ribbon around her neck and a fake wrist watch on her left hind leg, so the audience can see her leg until the last second, when she enters the cabinet. I say, "She is all dressed up like a bride" and that gets a big laugh for the good natured beast lumbers along and I believe she is the best natured elephant that ever lived. I never allowed a hook to be used, relying on block sugar to make her go through her stunt and she certainly is very fond of me.

She weighs over ten thousand pounds and is gentle as a kitten. Everything is in bright light; it is no "black art" and it is a wonderful mystery for an elephant to be manipulated, they move so slowly.

Houdini's runup of the illusion contains a few inaccuracies, probably purposely inserted, as they are of the sort that are commonly used when endeavoring to describe a magical effect without disclosing its secret. Such discrepancies are apparent to anyone used to reading "between the lines" of a magic catalog or a playbill, wherein everything seems utterly impossible until skillfully analyzed and may often remain baffling even then.

In this case Houdini "slipped one by" that might have fooled a magician, but would have been caught up by a naturalist. A 5-ton African elephant would stand eight feet high, so the elephant must have been much smaller or the cabinet a good deal larger than Houdini specified.

But there was nothing small about Jennie, as a photo of Houdini and the elephant plainly shows, with Jennie rearing to twice Houdini's height. So the cabinet must have well exceeded the "eight feet square" that Houdini so casually estimated.

This is evidenced by a report from a magical correspondent which appeared in the same issue of the *Sphinx* as Houdini's own account. The correspondent stated:

At the Hippodrome, I watched Houdini vanish an elephant...

The elephant was a big specimen ... and Houdini introduced him and made the elephant happy—and the rest of us envious—as he treated him to a lump of sugar. In fact, Houdini said the elephant was the cause of the sugar shortage!

Then an immense cabinet was wheeled on into which Mr. Jumbo shambled and without any protest permitted himself to be vanished. The Hippodrome being of such colossal size, only those sitting directly in front got the real benefit of the deception. The few hundred people sitting around me took Houdini's word for it that the "animile" had gone. We couldn't see into the cabinet at all!

This description was correct in every detail except the sex of the elephant. However, it requires further clarification. The Hippodrome's shape, as much as its size, made it difficult for most people to look through the Elephant Cabinet. The stage was not only large, it had an apron extending out into the auditorium so that the downstairs spectators formed a semicircle about it. Balcony patrons had their problems, too, as the "pitch" down to the stage was so steep that the top of the cabinet cut off any view of the interior when the front curtains were opened.

Now, let us peer into the cabinet itself and see how it would have fared under more ideal circumstances, or, to put it more simply, how it looked to those fortunate customers who watched it directly from the front.

Here is how they were benefited by the deception:

They saw a slightly oblong cabinet which was set side wall toward the audience, so that its curtained front end was toward one wing of the stage and the back, which consisted of a pair of split doors, was toward the other wing.

This, oddly, was the only fair and proper way to display the cabinet in the Hippodrome. It gave the people at the sides a chance to view the interior "before" the vanish, whereas the folks in the center would have the "after" look.

Houdini spread the "front" curtains and opened the "back" doors exactly as he stated, but remember, at that time, these were "faced" toward opposite wings. The curtains slid apart at the front of the cabinet.

The doors were split and opened in opposite directions at the back.

Jennie then strolled on stage, had her sugar with Houdini by the footlights along the apron and was ushered from there to the front of the cabinet, which she entered with due éclat. The curtains were then drawn shut at Houdini's order, and the two doors were closed at the back.

The front was then slowly but steadily turned straight toward the audience. Remember, the cabinet now contained some five tons of elephant—more or less—so it took a stage crew of a dozen men to engineer the task with the aid of a special block and tackle, much like a flock of tugboats warping an ocean liner into dock.

This took up some of the "seven or eight minutes" that Houdini mentioned as essential to the trick. By the time that was over, he was ready for the "two seconds" in which he opened the back and the front to show that the elephant was gone.

In those two seconds, all Houdini did was whisk the front curtains apart. He didn't have to rush around and open the back doors. That was already done, as far as needed or intended. Each half of the back door had an oval cutout in the edge, so that when closed, they showed a circular opening in the center. The audience saw through the cabinet and out the hole in the back.

Apparently the elephant had vanished; otherwise there would have been no unobstructed view. That, at least, was what people were supposed to think. Houdini won his point, as it was generally conceded that the elephant had somehow left the cabinet. But any chance that Jennie had been lowered through a trap was nullified on three counts:

First, most of the audience on the orchestra level could see beneath the cabinet, from the sides as well as the front, giving a continuously unobstructed view. Here, the wide angles of vision helped make the vanish convincing.

Second, no elevator large enough to carry Jennie's weight could have operated with sufficient speed, since most of the available time was spent in putting the cabinet into its final position, allowing only a few seconds before the climax.

Third, the illusion was presented over the huge tank containing a quarter of a million gallons of water, which served as a miniature lake in the Hippodrome spectacles. Later in the show Houdini did a submerged box escape in the tank, so most of the audience was aware of its presence.

How, then, did the elephant vanish and where did it actually go?

The answer was that it never left the cabinet. To begin with, the cabinet was much bigger than it looked, because the vastness of the Hippodrome stage "brought it down" to what seemed a normal or reasonable size. It must be remembered that this was at a time when many vaudeville bills featured illusionists who used curtain cabinets to produce or vanish anything from half a dozen people up to a piano or a caged lion.

So Houdini was simply operating on a mammoth scale before spectators accustomed to thinking in terms of "eight square feet" as about the largest a cabinet would be. It took a practiced eye to class the cabinet as "immense" and even then, its proportions were deceptive. One critic termed the cabinet "as big as a garage," which was practically an understatement, as it had to be that size even to receive the elephant, let alone vanish it. He should have specified a "two-car garage" to be closer to fact.

While the cabinet was being slowly swung frontward by the stage crew, who used a special block and tackle for the job, the trainer, who had gone into the cabinet with the elephant, was working his charge over to one side. There, the elephant took a longitudinal stance and a black interior curtain was pulled into place, matching the inside of the cabinet and effectually hiding the elephant.

When the front end curtains were drawn apart, the audience simply looked into a vast void, where nothing was visible, because there was no way it could be. That is, nothing could be seen except the circular opening at the back of the cabinet which immediately caught the eye and seemed to loom larger, the more it was studied.

It was something like looking into the opened interior of an old-fashioned box camera and through the lens beyond. People did see clear through the cabinet and the strong light coming in from the back opening gave the interior an imaginary perspective that minimized the extent of the surrounding darkness and at the same time added to its intensity.

The front curtain was widely bunched at the side where the elephant was hidden, thus helping the illusion all the more. There was sufficient space at the side for the elephant to stand there; but even if kneeling or reclining, its concealment was simple enough, once it was covered by a black drape that was totally swallowed in that Stygian darkness.

A prime phase of the deception lay in having the cabinet set sidewise at the outset, so that when the elephant entered, no one was able to compare its width with that of the cabinet front, which was much greater, that is, no one except persons at the extreme side of the orchestra, and even their view was restricted somewhat by the angle.

Houdini's insistence that it was no "black art" was a rather dubious disclaimer, for the illusion actually had the elements of the old time "Black Art Act," where in the entire stage has a black velvet background and any white object can be made to vanish or appear by simply covering or uncovering it with a black cloth of the same material.

Technically, though, Houdini had a point, because the Black Art setting demands a strong glare from the front and the term itself applies to a stage set rather than a cabinet. In "Spirit Cabinet" acts, however, blackness had been used to hide human "spooks" who were hooded in black costumes. So the Vanishing Elephant was, in a sense, a mammoth version of a "spook" cabinet.

The real novelty was the hole in the center of the back, giving a "look-through" that was practical only with a tremendous cabinet and at a distance possible only on a stage as huge as the Hippodrome's.

Otherwise it might have been too obvious or admitted too much light. As it was, the only problem was to keep the elephant clear of the hole in the back. That, of course, was automatic, once the elephant's side of the cabinet was properly closed off by the interior curtain. The dimensions were definitely deceiving, for one expert, who correctly pictured a side curtain or interior panel running from the front of the cabinet to the back, was still unable to believe that Jumbo's daughter could be confined in what he thought was such a limited space.

So he decided that maybe the cabinet had a mirror instead of a black partition, running from the edge of the opened front curtain back to the very middle of the hole in the back door. Thus people were supposed to see an upright semicircle, plus its own reflection, making a full circle in all.

All very good, except at the Hipp, with people looking into the cabinet at so many odd angles, a lot of viewers would have been looking squarely at the mirror and getting a reflection of the auditorium; while others, whose line of vision was close to parallel with the mirror itself, would have seen only part of a hole in the back of the cabinet.

Keeping Jennie safely behind such a mirror would have been a problem of its own and swinging such a huge and cumbersome appliance into place could have proved still more difficult. So we can count the mirror "out" because it was never "in."

One glaring error in many descriptions of Houdini's Elephant Cabinet was the claim that the audience looked through two circular openings, one in front, the other in back. This would mean that the cabinet had doors in front instead of curtains, but such was not the case. Other descriptions garbled it worse, trying to place the "peek holes" in the sides instead of the front and the back, which just didn't make sense at all. Considering the depth of the cabinet, a circular front opening would have to be very large in order to readily see the hole at the back. A front opening of the same size as the back wouldn't line up easily with it. The front of the cabinet had to be closed while Jennie was performing her gyrations inside. So the uncovering of a suitably sized circular front opening would mean taking off practically the entire door, if there had been one on the cabinet front.

But as we already know, there were no doors in front; there were curtains, as described by Houdini himself. Where, then, did the notion of front and back "circular holes" ever come from?

The answer is an interesting one, which has hitherto been almost overlooked.

Two years after Houdini presented the Vanishing Elephant a trick was invented called the "Phantom Tube," which sprang to immediate popularity among magicians. The Phantom Tube is of double construction with a tapering interior, so it can be shown apparently empty by letting people look through the large end. Silk handkerchiefs are then produced by drawing them out from the space between the walls.

Later on when magicians who had seen the Vanishing Elephant were asked how it was done, they would say: "You looked through the cabinet, the same as a Phantom Tube," or "It was built like a Phantom Tube with an opening at the back." Such statements were correct, but they gave a distorted idea of the overall appearance of the Elephant Cabinet.

Soon people were picturing it as a thing like a boxcar, much longer than it was wide, which left no place for the elephant if you looked through from the front. Actually, its squarish shape was the real secret of the mystery, a thing which many experts forgot if they had ever known it at all.

Assuming an elephant's length to be more than three times its width, it is quite obvious that if it walked straight into a square cabinet—as Houdini's elephant did—it could be packed over to one side, taking up less than one third of the cabinet's width when viewed from the front. Actually, one fourth would be a better estimate, as the cabinet had to be large enough to receive the elephant comfortably, with some footage to spare.

All animals are adaptable to concealment in one way or another, and elephants

Fig. 40. *Houdini at the Hippodrome, New York. One of the outstanding features of Charles Dillingham's Colossal Musical Revue, "Cheer Up."*

are no exception. Since Houdini had one at his disposal, it was simply a case of experimentation plus knowledge in illusion building to come up with a satisfactory result. Houdini definitely succeeded, for the act stayed on at the Hipp and its correct solution continued to puzzle many magical minds long afterward.

Other Elephant Vanishes

Along with the varied descriptions of the Elephant Cabinet used by Houdini at the Hippodrome, other methods of performing the Vanishing Elephant cropped up in the years that followed, most of them quite different in appearance and method from the illusion presented by Houdini.

Some of these were not only attributed to Houdini but were heralded as the actual vanish that he performed at the Hippodrome, so that in the years since Houdini's death many of the magicians and public alike have come to accept these versions as the one and only original.

That was further stimulated by the fact that the illusions were both workable and performed by noted stage magicians, so the Vanishing Elephant—in one form or another—has been witnessed quite often since Houdini's famed engagement at the old Hippodrome. However, there seems to have been a complete lull in pachydermatous prestidigitation during the eight years between Houdini's appearance at the Hipp in 1918 and his death in 1926.

This was quite understandable: Houdini had established something of a priority where the Vanishing Elephant was concerned, and he might have prevented anyone from showing such an illusion in vaudeville. He was also planning the full evening show which he finally took on the road in 1925 and was working at the time of his death a year later. The chance that Houdini might have put the Vanishing Elephant into his own big show was enough to forestall competition.

There were vanishing goats, ponies, donkeys, horses, camels, and even automobiles shown by illusionists of the early 1920s, but no elephants! It wasn't the cost of building or carrying the equipment that restrained them; it was the cost of fighting Houdini. Whether or not he was keeping the Vanishing Elephant in reserve to prove his show was "biggest," the world was never to find out.

But what the world did find out was that other magicians were eager and ready to come up with elephant effects, once Houdini wasn't there to stop them. Within a few years after Houdini's death, Carter and Nicola, two illusionists who toured the world, were each performing a Vanishing Elephant illusion, while Thurston, Houdini's big rival on the American stage, introduced an "Appearing Elephant" that lasted only a week, when Delhi, the elephant, caught cold and died.

Carter had problems with his elephant, too, but Nicola featured the Vanishing Elephant in vaudeville theaters throughout the United States, so many persons may recall having seen an elephant disappear on a fully lighted stage. But unless they can peg that occasion as far back as 1918 and on the stage of the New York Hippodrome, they didn't see Houdini do it.

All the elephants, except Houdini's Jennie, were of a pygmy breed, so they could be transported easily and could be vanished—or produced—on a stage of average size. So as we delve further into the realm of elephantine enchantment, let it be remembered that we are dealing with peewee pachyderms, under two tons in weight, rather than Houdini's sweetheart, five-ton Jennie.

The Double Cabinet

The type of cabinet which has been confused with the one Houdini used has various modifications, which will be discussed in brief. In its simplest form, it is a square, or more precisely, cubical cabinet consisting of top, back, side walls, and open front, where a curtain is drawn as soon as the elephant has entered.

After a brief interval—perhaps no more than a few seconds—the curtain is whisked open and the elephant has vanished. The top and the sides are then swung wide, to give everyone a full view of the interior. The light, portable construction of the cabinet adds to the effect of the vanish.

Actually, two cabinets are needed for this disappearance. In the simple and somewhat primitive form just described, the second cabinet, which is of solid construction but smaller in size, is situated directly in back of the large cabinet, which is the only one the audience sees.

The smaller or hidden cabinet has no front, other than the back of the large cabinet itself. This is divided into four panels and the center pair either slide apart or swing open, allowing the elephant to march right through to the cozy little cabinet at the rear.

This takes place immediately after the curtained front of the big cabinet is closed. Once the elephant has gone through and the back panels are again shut, the cue is given for the vanish. The front curtain is whipped open, the hinged portions of the big cabinet are spread wide and the show is over. If the rear panels are made to swing instead of slide, they should open forward into the large cabinet where the space is ample. The hidden cabinet is just about the elephant's size, so the front, or visible cabinet has to be considerably larger to conceal the one behind it.

A cabinet of this type could never have been used at the Hippodrome because of the angles, both from the sides and from above. The big cabinet would have had to be far out of proportion to hide the little one and with a full-sized elephant being featured in the trick, it would have needed to be still larger.

The "Double Cabinet" was more of the type used by Nicola, but it had disadvantages too, on stages that were too shallow. Then, the cabinet had to be set so close to the backdrop that it looked as though the elephant walked right on through and out the stage door. Nicola's vanish was frequently criticized on that count, but he regarded the Vanishing Elephant as worth more than its weight in publicity and therefore was willing to present it even under adverse conditions.

In that, Nicola was definitely following Houdini's own pattern, as the original Hippodrome vanish was more of a ballyhoo than a mystery.

Another Elephant Vanish

Within a few years after Houdini's death, another version of the Vanishing Elephant was publicized as the original Hippodrome method. The authority for that claim was a backstage mechanic who had formerly worked for Houdini. In this form the illusion is shown on the open stage, with no cabinet whatever. This proves that it was not the trick presented at the Hippodrome, for there a cabinet was definitely utilized. An interesting point, however, is that Houdini may very possibly have experimented with this or a similar type of vanish, as his own comments at the time of the Hippodrome engagement indicate.

First, a description of the vanish: The elephant is brought on stage and stands sidewise toward the audience at about stage center, but well back from the footlights. A huge net, or mesh, is lowered in front of the elephant, which can still be plainly seen through the openwork.

Next, a curtain is dropped, briefly covering the net and thus hiding the elephant. The curtain immediately falls away and people find themselves staring in amazement through the meshwork, for in that mere moment the elephant has vanished, leaving empty space behind the net!

Now for the explanation, as well as to the possible "link" between this vanish and Houdini's:

When the curtain rolls down in front of the big net, another roll of cloth simultaneously comes down behind it. This hidden cloth, which falls unobserved under cover of the curtain, exactly matches the backdrop just beyond the elephant. Hence, when the curtain is gone, so is the elephant, as the matching cloth cuts off any view of the elephant, yet gives the audience what still appears to be an unobstructed view of the backdrop itself.

That is the reason for the net. If the masking should be completely "open"—as in a large frame— the eye would be likely to detect the difference between it and the backdrop, either in terms of distance, color, or even the shading.

But when viewed through the mesh, any such difference is less appreciable and therefore safer from detection.

The farther front the trick is shown, the better the effect and in the case of an animal as large as an elephant, there definitely must be a considerable space between the net and the backdrop. Here again there is danger of the masking being noticed, even despite the net, unless a dark background is used. The darkest of all, of course, is black, which would put the illusion into the "black art" class.

Referring back to Houdini's comments on his Vanishing Elephant we find the double mention: "No special background ... No black art." Since both are involved in the type of vanish where the net and masking cloth are used, it is logical to suppose that Houdini did consider such a method but rejected it in favor of the cabinet that he finally built. Regardless of the comparative merits of such methods, the restraining factor was still the limitation of the Hippodrome's stage. Unless the illusion had been set far back, people would have seen past the edges of the masking curtain. The trick just couldn't be done that way at the Hipp.

How the "masking" type of vanish came to be mixed with Houdini's Vanishing Elephant was something that occurred as follows:

In the mid-1920s, Thurston presented a "Vanishing Horse" illusion that worked on the principle described. The horse was hoisted up behind a hanging net and vanished there. A few years later Carter adapted the Vanishing Horse into a similar illusion with an elephant. So the Vanishing Elephant later attributed to Houdini by the former stage mechanic was actually a version performed by Carter.

Elephant Vanish in Circus Ring

Prior to Houdini's engagement at the Hippodrome, a noted inventor and builder of illusions, Guy Jarrett, planned a Vanishing Elephant for the giant stage, but his elaborate production was unfortunately shelved and never put on there.

As part of the production, Jarrett planned to vanish a small elephant as well as a large one.

The second disappearance, that of the smaller elephant, was to take place under most exacting conditions. Apparently, Jarrett never went ahead with his idea, but a similar vanish was later described in detail by Jean Boullet, an ingenious French magical inventor, who proposed it for presentation in the middle of a circus ring:

A small elephant is marched beneath a rectangular framework, or canopy, where curtains are promptly lowered around it, the elephant's feet showing on the platform where it stands. The feet, too, are finally hidden and a group of Hindu assistants approach from the fringes of the ring.

At the magician's order, the assistants whip open the curtains, sliding them to the corners of the cabinet, folding them there to reveal every square foot of the interior. Except for the flimsy curtains, nothing is left but a skeleton framework, the elephant having completely vanished.

The elephant is a "two-man prop," consisting of a pair of assistants in an elephant costume, the one sort of animal which, according to Jarrett, can be successfully imitated, an opinion with which Boullet evidently concurred. As soon as the "elephant" is within the cabinet, its occupants divest themselves of the clumsy costume and pack its parts inside the curtains. All portions of the costume are pliable or compressible, so when the Hindu assistants rapidly gather the curtains to the corners of the cabinet, they can easily bundle up the pieces of the costume inside them. As an alternative, the remains of the "elephant" could be stowed in a double floor of the shallow platform, by the two men who impersonated the midget mastodon.

These two "inside" assistants are dressed exactly like the crew of Hindus who invade the cabinet and demolish it. There should be enough of those outsiders so that in the general rush and rapid excitement, the presence of two more will not be noticed or suspected. They start opening the curtains all at once, helping each other and finally separating to return outside the ring, while the audience still gapes in astonishment at the blank platform.

The Orange Tree

THIS ILLUSION WAS PRESENTED with great success by William Robinson, who appeared in Oriental robes under the name of Chung Ling Soo and hoodwinked the vaudeville public of Great Britain into believing that he was a genuine Chinese conjurer. Robinson was unfortunately killed while performing the "Bullet Catching Trick" in a London theater in 1918 and several years later Houdini revived the "Orange Tree" and made it a feature of his full evening show.

Inasmuch as Houdini's presentation of the illusion had some distinct points of novelty the Orange Tree belongs in a collection of his choicest secrets. As usually performed, it was simply a transformation. A girl stood on a circular platform, a huge cone was lowered over her and immediately raised again. Instead of the girl, the audience saw an orange tree, bearing ripe fruit. Oranges were plucked and tossed to the audience and, during the course of that procedure, the missing girl made her reappearance somewhere in the theater.

The "orange tree" was an artificial specimen, very realistic in appearance, but so thick with imitation foliage that people failed utterly to see the "trick" of its construction.

Actually, the branches and leaves are formed about an inner cone and are of a "springy" nature so that they spread out the moment that the thin outer shell is hauled clear.

In the usual presentation, therefore, the girl stood on the platform, the cone was lowered over her, and catches were released so that when the "cone" was lifted, the "tree" spread itself into sight and the girl was completely hidden within its conical center. She remained there while the magician plucked the oranges and meanwhile, her twin or double made a well-timed appearance somewhere in the audience.

That was all right for Chung Ling Soo, whose assistants all had Chinese make-up and looked enough alike to deceive the audience into thinking that the same girl had returned. Also, he used the Orange Tree in vaudeville, where the tempo of the tricks was faster than in a full evening show.

Houdini did not use twins; he purposely avoided doing so, because so many stage magicians resorted to that device that it had become fairly well known or at least suspected by most audiences. People who saw the Houdini show looked in vain for twins; none of the girls resembled each other at all closely. For the Orange Tree, moreover, he used a petite mademoiselle who spoke with a French accent and definitely established her individualism.

Here, then, was how Houdini's presentation looked:

The girl was introduced and took her place on the circular platform which was mounted on legs, giving a clear view beneath. The huge cone was lowered over her by chains and was hauled away at Houdini's command, the girl being gone, with no sign yet of anything else.

Suspicion followed the cone on the assumption that the girl had gone up inside it, but Houdini dispelled that by having assistants lower it sufficiently to swing the lower end of the cone toward the audience, where he proved conclusively that it was empty, having the spotlight thrown directly into its interior, which he probed with a long stick, showing that mirrors or hidden compartments were out of the question.

The cone was then swung on to the stand again; this time, when it was lifted, the audience expected to see the girl, back again. Instead, they were nonplused by the sight of the colorful orange tree, materialized from nothingness. Houdini called for the house lights and, as they flashed on, the missing mademoiselle came dashing down the aisle, shouting *"Je suis ici! Je suis ici!"* She rushed up the steps to the stage, where Houdini received her and both took a bow in the shadow of the amazing orange tree.

How Houdini maneuvered all this was puzzling to many magicians and here, probably for the first time, is the detailed explanation:

In addition to the conventional Orange Tree and its double cone, Houdini used a platform deep enough to conceal the girl. The platform did not look suspicious, because it had to be a strong one in order to take the weight of the huge cone. That, too, demanded a platform of considerable diameter, so the platform's depth was minimized in comparison to its overall width.

The special platform had a trap in its thin top, and Houdini purposely used a slender and somewhat diminutive girl in the illusion. The orange tree was designed to take a girl of fairly sizable proportions, so by reversing the accepted rule, Houdini allowed his petite assistant ample room to operate.

The moment the girl was covered by the cone, she stooped down, opened the trap, and coiled inside the double platform, letting the trap close over her. This was done quite rapidly so that suspicion followed the cone when it was lifted. As Houdini ordered the cone swung outward by two assistants, the platform was in the way, so another pair obligingly moved it from the center of the stage, so that Houdini could take his own stand there.

As the glare of the spotlight was focused into the empty cone and Houdini supplied dramatic action by taking a long pole from an assistant and thrusting it up into the cone, the rest of the stage was in comparative darkness. Nobody noticed that the other assistants took the platform well out of the way by sliding it clear to the wing of the stage.

There the girl emerged from the platform and hurried out the stage door or through an inside passage to the front of the theater. Her getaway was a matter of moments, and by the time Houdini had convinced the audience that the cone was really empty and was turning to call for the platform, the assistants were already sliding it in his direction.

The replacement of the cone on the platform took enough more time for the girl to be at the back of the audience when Houdini called for the chains to lift it anew. Thus, while the audience was fascinated by the sudden appearance of the orange tree, Houdini could call almost immediately for house lights, giving the girl her cue to start down the aisle to the stage.

Well timed and properly cued, as it invariably was, this presentation of the Orange Tree was highly effective, but that was chiefly due to Houdini's ability as a showman. He commanded such full attention that most people never realized that the platform was rolled more than a short way from the center of the stage, so they failed utterly to guess how the girl made her getaway.

Houdini's Radio Illusion

THIS WAS AN INTRIGUING illusion that Houdini introduced in his full evening show, which was presented at the time when radio was coming into popularity. Actually, it was not a trick involving a radio, but a somewhat unusual type of production cabinet.

A large, rectangular table was shown on the stage and on top of it was a huge version of a radio cabinet of the 1920s, about six feet wide and proportionately high and deep. It was recognizable as a radio cabinet because it was equipped with the usual dials, which of course were oversized.

The table, though standing on high legs, was skirted with a deep cloth that observers naturally regarded with more than slight suspicion. Houdini promptly raised the cloth all around the edges of the table and looked through from the back, using a long pole to flip the cloth and prove it innocent.

He then had assistants lower the front and the back of the mammoth radio, showing it to be nothing but a large box, except for a few tubes, wires, and other radio equipment. After the cabinet was closed, Houdini ended the last vestiges of doubt by removing the circling cloth entirely to show that the table top was simply a thin planking on which the cabinet was mounted.

Houdini turned the dials, and music came from the giant radio. It ended abruptly when the cabinet popped open and a girl appeared from within.

The secret lay in the table, which had what magicians term a "bellows top" consisting of two thin slabs, with several inches of strong cloth folded in between the edges, so the lower "top" can be let down to a set distance, which in this case was less than the depth of the loose drape that skirted the table.

When Houdini first lifted the drape and showed "all clear" beneath the table, the girl was in the radio cabinet. He dropped the skirting cloth, and the girl promptly went through a trap in the upper portion of the double top. The lower section dropped far enough for the trap to close, but not so far that it could be seen below the drape.

The radio cabinet was then dismantled, shown empty, and put together. The girl came up through the trap and the lower portion of the top was brought up to its original position. By then Houdini was ready to remove the cloth entirely, which he did. The girl then made her magical appearance the moment that the music was cut off, coming from a cabinet which had clearly been shown empty and which was now resting on a thin-topped, undraped table.

Most of the audience remembered the table as they finally saw it, making this an excellent production, thanks to Houdini's brisk showmanship.

The Giant Card Star

SOME OF THE OLDER TRICKS in modern magic are still the best, because of a natural audience appeal that has enabled them to survive the years. Gradually, however, the most enchanting effect can be lost, when the apparatus itself becomes antiquated and the method appears correspondingly obvious to persons accustomed to a newer brand of mystery.

The element of surprise still holds, but it must in some way leave observers baffled, hence it is often essential to improve old effects, or else abandon them. Such was true of the "Card Star," an old-timer wonder that had long outlived its original glory and was all but forgotten when Houdini revived it and turned it into a really excellent effect.

The Card Star is a metal star, which in the old form was mounted on an upright rod extending from an ornamental base. This stands on a table or is held by an assistant, while the magician has spectators select five or six cards from a pack, according to the number of points on the star that he happens to use.

That done, the pack is thrown at the star and in the flurry of flying pasteboards, the chosen cards suddenly appear, each on a different point of the star. Some of the old "professors" of the old prestidigitorial art were wont to ram the chosen cards into a big-muzzled pistol and fire it at the Card Star. In any event, the result was the same, the chosen cards appeared on the points.

The Card Star, with all its charm, had two decided disadvantages. Its center portion was larger than a playing card, so it soon dawned on more observant audiences that the cards could easily be hidden there prior to their arrival on the star points.

In fact, that was exactly how it worked. Behind each point, there was a short rod, operating on a spring hinge about two inches from the actual point and with a special clip on the outer end. Cards were placed endwise in these clips and the rods were folded back one by one, behind the center of the star, each card holding down the one before.

The final card was held in place by a short lever projecting up from the shaft on which the fancy star was mounted. The lever could be drawn down either by a cord running off through the base to a hidden assistant, or by a small button in the back of the shaft, which was pressed down by the person holding the star.

The result was that at the right instant, the cards were released and the rods sprang outward in such rapid succession that the result was almost simultaneous, each card appearing suddenly on a star point. But nice though it looked, it wasn't "magic" to anyone who guessed where the cards came from, even though he couldn't have described the exact mechanism.

The other bad feature was that as theaters grew from small halls into large auditoriums, the effect of the Card

Star was lost, because the cards couldn't be distinguished by persons at the back of the audience. So the trick became outmoded until Houdini came up with his new and sensational "Giant Card Star."

The term "giant" applied to the cards, not to the star. Houdini's Card Star was no larger than the old type, in fact it looked exactly the same, which was the deceiving factor. For Houdini's pack consisted of the newly introduced Jumbo Playing Cards that were four times the size of the usual variety! Houdini showed the giant pack and invited members of the audience to call the names of playing cards at random. He repeated the first five that were called off and the Card Star was brought on to the stage and hung by ribbons, so that it was completely isolated. Houdini threw the giant pack against the star and the five chosen cards appeared, each half the size of the star itself, as long as the distance from the center to the point on which the card arrived. A real baffler, indeed!

Even magicians were puzzled by Houdini's Giant Star, which literally hinged on a very ingenious device. Houdini had an entire set of giant cards made up—fifty-two in all—from thin metal. Each card was divided into three crosspieces which were fitted with tiny hinges and strong springs, so that it could be folded into one third its size, but when released, would spring out to full form.

The metal cards were so mechanically perfect that the divisions could not be noticed more than a few feet away. An assistant had the entire set laid out backstage and when people in the audience called names of cards, Houdini repeated them so the assistant could hear them and fix them in back of the star.

As each card was placed, it was folded into thirds, so that the giant cards occupied little more space than would have been required for those of normal size. The release lever that held the folding cards in place was connected to an ornamental knob or button on the front of the star and in the exact center.

Thus, when the star was brought on stage, it could be hung as described and when Houdini threw the pack of regular Jumbo cards against it, their weight was sufficient to spring the release by simply striking the knob. The folding cards instantly appeared on the star points, opening on the way.

The whole effect, the impact of the pack, the scattering of all the cards, except the chosen ones, which appeared on a swaying star that was obviously too small to hide them, was

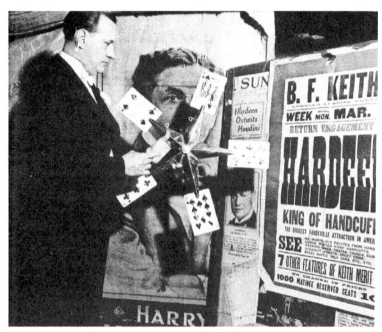

Fig. 41. *Douglas Geoffrey (Hardeen Jr.)*
and the Houdini Card Star, 1945.

magical indeed. Houdini introduced this striking mystery in his big show, and it promptly became one of the most talked about features in his performance.

The Giant Card Star, incidentally, provides an interesting commentary for magical historians. When Houdini published his *Unmasking of Robert-Houdin* he criticized his esteemed predecessor for having claimed certain tricks that others had invented long before.

In short, Robert-Houdin was not the originator that he claimed to be, at least not according to Houdini's findings.

Defenders of Robert-Houdin have said that Houdini was mistaken. The tricks that Robert-Houdin presented as originations were improvements of older effects, so much better that they were new in their own right. Houdini had confused the old with the new, to the undeserved discredit of RobertHoudin.

Very probably that was true. If ever poetic justice won its case, it was with the Card Star.

To say that Houdini, in the year 1925, introduced a trick as "new" that had been outmoded in 1890 would be disparaging indeed, if taken literally.[3] Unfortunately, it could be taken just that way, due to references to Houdini's working the "old" Card Star.

Actually, Houdini's Card Star was not only "new," it was unique. Like his namesake, Houdin, he left his indelible imprint on whatever he did. Both, very appropriately, forgot the "old" when they produced the "new" and assumed that posterity would duly credit them. But posterity is not always that kind; or perhaps it just does not care.

------

3 Professor Hoffmann describes the Card Star as the "Fairy Star" in his momentous Modern Magic, which appeared in 1878. But in More Magic, the sequel published in 1890, he supplies a newer method, titled the "Cabalistic Star," to show that the old method was obsolete even then.

The Buried Box Escape

DURING THE two seasons that Houdini appeared with his full evening magic show, he demonstrated the test of being buried alive or kept in a box under water during a period of approximately one hour. In doing this, Houdini counteracted the claims of self-styled "miracle workers" who attributed the feat to Oriental parentage plus autohypnosis. Houdini openly declared that the only requisites for this demonstration were self-confidence and endurance, for the air supply in the box used was sufficient to sustain the performer for a period considerably longer than his imprisonment. It is interesting to learn that Houdini considered this trick long before he presented it, and was familiar with the fact that a person could exist for a surprisingly long period before his air supply was exhausted. His notes refer to the "buried-alive man secret." The notes read:

> A large box about the size of a large kitchen table. The man enters, his mouth stuffed with cotton, likewise his nostrils.
>
> He has a hood placed over him, with the eyes cut out; then a longer hood over that which falls over his shoulders.

He lies down in sand with his arms under his chest; his knees drawn under him. His back is upwards. The secret is that the space made with his knees allows him to have enough air to live fifteen to thirty minutes. Wet damp sand allows longer time ...

When the man takes his place in the bottom of the box there is some sand already, and he is covered with about 1,500 to 3,000 pounds of sand.

A challenge test is to build a box with rubber band and a cover put on, which is pressed down so as to make it airtight.

I presume that with oxygen one could live much longer.

In the act of lying down, the cotton is pushed out of the mouth; it then lies against the nose in the second hood, which enables the man to breathe.

Knowing that he could breathe comfortably in an empty box—the way in which he eventually demonstrated the feat—

Fig. 42. *"Buried Alive" poster prepared for Houdini's last season.*

Houdini planned a highly spectacular escape, which he describes and explains thus:

> Get nailed into a packing case; lowered into a six-foot hole; then the earth or sand shoveled on same.
>
> Box can be made to work on side, so that I could worm my way out towards the air.
>
> Must have the hole in which box is buried large so that I do not have to strike the solid earth, but can work my way out through the sand or earth that has been dropped on box that contains me. Must be tried out to see how much air I have with me.

Penciled notations follow the typed explanation:

> I tried out "Buried Alive" in Hollywood, and nearly (?) did it. Very dangerous; the weight of the earth is killing.

Earlier notes on this escape were written by Houdini while on board a North German Lloyd steamer. They are dated "June 14, 1911, near Cherbourg." In these notes he provides for a special type of end trap in the box, which appears to have two loose boards, hinged together and held by a catch at the top of the box. A release of the catch permits the boards to drop inward, one upon the other, thus allowing a large opening for the escape. The notes also provide for bolts to hold the boards in position; when these are released from the inside, the trap is free to work.

Houdini realized that his exit from the box would be but the first part of this difficult escape, and it is obvious that he intended not to be handicapped by any limitations in the trap. Coming out into earth presented a tremendous problem when compared with the familiar escape of emerging into water. In planning his exit from the box and then through loose earth at the sides, Houdini chose the only possible method of escape.

Any attempt to raise the cover of the box and the earth above it, even with a powerful jack, would prove hopeless and there is no indication that Houdini even considered such a method. An escape by raising the cover and thus dislodging the loose earth above would be just about as practical as an exit through the bottom of the box!

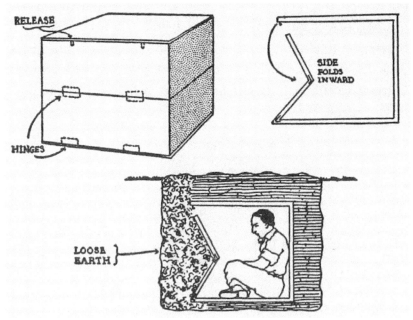

Fig. 43. *Construction of the box*
used in the Buried Box Escape, with
arrangement of loose earth.

Pillory Escapes

Pillory "A"

PILLORY "A" is very ingenious. The lower half is mounted on two posts and is made in two sections. From the inside of one post, a cut runs to a wrist-hole, then curves down below the neck-hole, and comes up to the other wrist-hole and down to the inside of the other post. A secret hinge holds it to the post at one end; a catch holds it to the post at the other.

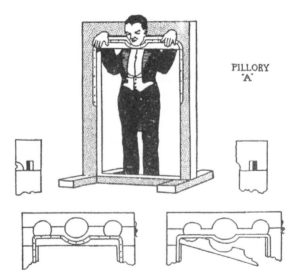

Fig. 44. *Explanatory diagrams of Pillory "A" Escape.*

194

To hide the cut, the posts and the lower part of the pillory are decorated with a brass binding which follows the break, just touching the lower edges of the wrist-holes. Fake rivets in the brass binding reinforce the deception. The performer releases himself by kicking the post that has the catch. This releases the catch and the lower section of the pillory breaks apart, allowing ample space for the performer to remove his head and hands. The apparatus is easily restored to its original condition.

The Torture Pillory

The Torture Pillory is an excellent escape trick, which may be recommended for its case of operation as well as for its effectiveness. The plans for this apparatus were given to Houdini and were contained in his notes.

The pillory is mounted on an upright rod or pedestal. It consists of three frames joined together, each frame opening on a hinge. the escape artist places his wrists in the end holes and his neck in the center. the upper sections are closed and are locked with padlocks which may be supplied by the audience.

Despite the fact that the pillory has stood a brief examination by a committee from the audience, the escapist leaves it very quickly after it has been covered by a cabinet. The pillory is shown again, with all the locks in place and no trace of trickery.

The diagrams reveal the secret of the pillory. Each frame opens two ways—either by the hinges, as the spectators know, or by sliding upward. The brass strips at the side of each frame are really grooves into which the upper portions fit. The brass strips at the top are not connected with the strips at the sides, although they fit so closely that they appear to be tightly joined.

In order that the pillory may stand a reasonable amount of inspection, the grooves at the sides of the frame are fitted with curved springs. The upper portions of the frames press against the springs and virtually lock in place.

The escape artist effects his release by exerting pressure in an upward direction. He is in an excellent position to raise his head and force out the frame which binds his neck. He then attends to the frames that hold his wrists. Following his escape, he pushes the frames back into position, so that they are clamped between the springs.

This is an excellent pillory escape, as it is sure and simple in operation. Most escapes of this type depend on some trickery in the locks or the hinges and those are the parts that the committee is sure to examine. The very ingenuity of this device is the important point that prevents the examiners from discovering the secret.

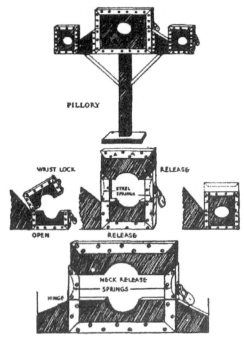

Fig. 45. *The Torture Pillory and details of its construction.*

Underwater Escapes

Rubber Bag and Glass Box

OF ALL THE escapes explained in Houdini's notes, the rubber bag and glass box most aptly prove that a very simple trick can be made into a spectacular mystery if properly presented. Everything in this trick is designed to mislead the audience: the objects that are used seem free of trickery because of their construction; it appears that the escape must require a long time to accomplish, whereas it is very quick; and finally, the escape seems to be full of complications, while actually it is comparatively easy of execution.

The conditions under which the performer is imprisoned are novel and unusual. He is placed in a bag made entirely of rubber, which will pass close examination. Then, the top of the bag is tied with rope and knotted by members of the committee. In the sides of the rubber bag are two small holes; these are fitted with valves, so that two long pieces of rubber hose may be attached. A watertight box is then required. The committee has been examining this, and the inspection shows that it is a glass aquarium with wooden posts and bottom, sheets of glass set in a wooden frame with a hinged top provided with a hasp and staple at the other side.

The bag containing the performer is placed in the glass box, and water is introduced with a fire hose. As soon as the water reaches a point above the bag, an assistant begins to let air into one hose from a tank; the other hose passes off to a post, and allows bad air to escape. the cover has two cutouts, one on each side, so that when the glass box is filled with water and the top is closed, nothing interferes with the rubber hose.

Then the box is padlocked, and a cabinet covers the box, leaving the assistant with the air tank outside.

By this time the audience is deeply interested. Here is a double problem. The performer must escape from the rubber bag and then make his exit from the box. Meanwhile he is dependent on the hose for air. To escape from the bag first will leave him without his air supply, and he may not have time to work free from the box; to escape from the box first seems quite impossible, for the rubber bag interferes with the performer's actions.

Yet, that is the way he intends to go about it. For when the curtains are thrown aside, the performer is not only free but dry. The glass box is locked and may be examined; the rubber bag is inside, still knotted, and puffed with air!

From the standpoint of presentation, this trick is excellent. It is one that people will talk about; it is therefore a real box office attraction. Furthermore, the man who does it has a much easier task than the audience supposes, and to a performer of Houdini's ability, the trick would be nothing more than a simple routine. At the same time, this is an escape designed for a showman, and Houdini's extensive notes on the trick prove that he recognized its great possibilities.

Analyzing this escape, we observe that the performer must release himself from the glass box before attending to the rubber bag. The release from the box must be sure and easy, yet well concealed, for the performer is unquestionably handicapped by being in the bag. Hence Houdini states that the top must come up away from the frame so that by simply standing up, the cover is raised. "This," he wrote, "can be cleverly concealed."

First Method

The glass is attached to the top by a brass binding which is heavy at the corners, that is, the glass simply rests on the wooden frame, and the brass holds it in position. Bolts pass through the brass and enter the wood.

These bolts go into holes that have been made in the wood, hence the glass is held firmly to the top, but the bolts are removable. They appear to serve the purpose of screws, fastened into the wood itself. The top thus stands careful examination, especially as the spectators in the committee are devoting most of their attention to the lower part of the frame, where it fits on the framework of the box. There is no indication of the bolts inside the box; they cannot be operated from there; hence no one worries about them. The persons examining the box are easily convinced that the glass part is firmly in place. The performer cannot reach the outside of the box. This is where the assistants play an important part. It is necessary for them to move the box slightly so that a cabinet may be set over it. They naturally take hold of the top corners of the box, and, their fingers finding the bolts, draw the bits of iron back from the wooden holes. the bolts, it may be observed, are not necessarily removable. They cannot come all the way out. Slots from the brass binding down will enable them to slide up with the binding when the ends of the bolts do not engage the holes that are deep in the woodwork.

There may be several bolts at each corner; all may work free (either by slots or by faked bolt-heads) except one key bolt at each corner; these hold the glass and the binding firmly enough to pass inspection. Thus, when the performer stands up in the rubber bag, he can lift off the glass and its broad brass binding and carefully set it alongside the box, using his hands through the rubber bag.

Second Method

This release is in the hasp on the outside of the box. the staple is on the box; the hasp portion is on the cover. There are no inside connections, but the staple itself is operated in a neat mechanical fashion. Pulling on it will not disengage it from the box; spreading it will do the trick. Instead of using a padlock, an examined bolt and nut are used to hold the hasp to the staple.

These are placed in position. The bolt is wedge shaped and is forced down tightly by an assistant. This makes the fastening appear secure; it also spreads the staple automatically, and when the performer presses against the top of the box, the staple comes out, allowing the cover to be raised. Thus the entire cover of the box is solid and will stand any amount of examination; after the performer is out, a slight loosening of the bolt allows him to put the staple back in its original position. An alternate type of staple is a metal fitting that goes in the woodwork of the box. This is held by strong springs or fastenings, and ordinary pulling will not remove it.

When the performer presses firmly against the front of the cover, he pulls the staple clear of the woodwork.

Third Method

This plan, which Houdini considered probably the best, reverts to the extreme top of the cover, where the glass is bound into the box. The binding is held to the woodwork by hidden catches set in the woodwork. Bolts or screws through the binding either are free in the wood (by slots) or do not enter it. Yet the catches hold the binding securely, and there is no way in which they can be discovered or removed by the committee. These catches are actuated by little levers in the woodwork; the levers are horizontal and end in plugs set in vertical holes. On the framework of the box are pins that correspond with these holes. The obvious purpose of the pins and holes is to set the cover squarely on the box and hold it there so that padlocks may be attached to hasps and staples on all sides. Everything undergoes a rigid examination before the trick, for the glass and its framework are actually secure to the top of the cover. But as soon as the cover is fitted into position, the pins automatically operate the hidden catches, and the glass and framework may be pushed upward. The framework should be a tight fit, requiring a certain amount of pressure to free it. After escaping, the performer simply puts the glass and framework on again. As soon as the cabinet is removed, the locks are examined and taken off; then the assistants lift the cover and offer it for another examination.

The catches, having springs, are back in their original position, and the entire top is in perfect condition.

The Bag Escape

Escaping from the bag is an important item; the performer accomplishes this by untying the knots through the bag itself. The bag is made of thin rubber, and the knots can be very effectively handled. Houdini made little mention of this item, for untying knots through cloth or rubber offered him no difficulty. The supplying of a short length of rope makes it impossible to tie intricate knots, and the performer can retie the bag after he is out of it. Yet the use of the bag is extremely effective, especially because of the water. It makes a good box trick into an extraordinary one, and the bag escape and the tank escape are an excellent combination when worked together.

Of course the performer does not replace the parts of the glass box until he has released himself from the bag. He puts the bag into the box before making the box as secure as in the beginning, and being free from the bag, he has no difficult operations. It is also essential that the bag should be tied in a regular manner so that no difference will be detected by the committee; furthermore, the knots are wet and are not so easy to handle as dry knots. But well tied with square knots,

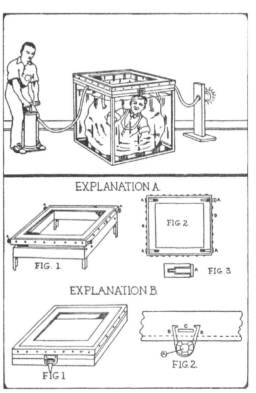

Fig. 46. *The rubber bag and the glass box.*

the bag will unfailingly satisfy the usual stage committee. As the preparations for the trick are rather elaborate and lengthy, the time allowed for this work is too short to permit delayed tying. In an emergency the performer may simply cut the rope with a sharp-pointed instrument and replace the old one with a new rope, covering the small opening in the rubber; or he can destroy the bag itself by cutting it or ripping it, replacing it with another bag tied exactly like the original. A duplicate bag and rope are therefore items of equipment to be concealed in the performer's cabinet.

The Crystal Water Casket

This is one of the most spectacular of all escapes. Consider a man imprisoned in a massive casket entirely filled with water and secured from the outside with genuine locks and massive straps, the walls and the top of the casket made of glass! The escape must be effected within a very few minutes, and escape seems impossible, for alert committee men may examine and seal the contrivance. Yet Houdini not only planned such a formidable device; he devised an ingenious method of getting out of it. The casket as the audience sees it is a strong wooden framework that supports sides of clear glass. A heavy cover fits on the casket; the sides of the cover are of glass, and so is the top. Both parts may be carefully inspected. Brass trimmings are on the edges, and the casket and cover are watertight. There is a certain peculiarity of the cover that serves a definite purpose. The sheet of glass on the top has a hole in the center. This hole is bound with metal and connected to the brass rim of the cover by flat bars both above and below the glass.

The casket is filled with water, and the performer appears in a bathing suit. Then he enters the casket and stands there with his head and shoulders out of water. The cover is lifted and set on the casket. It has a close-fitting downward flange that goes over the top edges of the casket and makes the whole affair watertight. Each side of the cover is supplied with a large mechanical lock which operates perfectly. These locks are thoroughly examined by the committee, and they pass inspection. They are inaccessible from within the cabinet. But to render the contrivance doubly secure, there are two staples on each side of the cover and corresponding staples on each side of the casket. As these staples are horizontal, the committee men can run heavy straps through them. Thus there are four straps, two in each direction, passing over and under the casket, which is mounted slightly to permit the passage of the straps. No effort is spared to make these straps tight, and they are buckled at the bottom of the cabinet. Their purpose is evident. Should the locks fail to hold the cover, the straps would still be an insurmountable barrier, for the lip or flange of the cover is too deep to allow the performer to reach through by pressing the cover upward.

The heavy straps are virtually unyielding; pressure can stretch them but a fraction of an inch. The only opening into the casket is the hole in the center of the cover; it is so small that the performer can merely put his arm through. But a hemispherical cap is designed to fit over it, and this fastens down to solid bolts or clamps that are thoroughly inspected and approved by the committee.

When the escapist is in the casket and the cover is on with the straps and the locks firmly secured, a funnel is inserted in the small hole in the center of the top, and water is poured in through a hose. The closed casket is watertight; hence the water level rises, and the performer, who has moved to a corner, is entirely immersed, with no possibility of obtaining air, for the water comes to the very top. Then the hemispherical cover is clamped on the hole; the bolts or clamps work quickly, so that the prison is sealed within a few seconds. Curtains are drawn about the apparatus, and the audience realizes that the performer is in a most precarious position. Three or four minutes seem the maximum time permissible for this escape, due to the lack of air within the casket; and the performer has lost a few precious seconds in the closing of the hole in the top. As the minutes go by, the spectators become tense and wonder what is going on inside the curtains, for this escape carries a real element of danger. Suddenly the curtains are thrown aside and there stands the performer, dripping with water. The casket is still locked and strapped; the water level has dropped because the performer is no longer within. The committee steps forward to inspect the apparatus. Nothing has been changed; everything is secure. The casket may be opened if desired, and an inspection of the interior will show nothing amiss.

There is a certain similarity between the crystal water casket and the glass box from which the performer escapes while in a rubber bag, but in the crystal casket quick escape is much more essential and the apparatus is much heavier and more formidable.

The first thing to consider is the spot where the performer makes his exit. This is at the extreme top of the cover. As in the glass box, the glass lifts off with the brass binding. This part of the apparatus must be secure when the committee examines it; yet it must be capable of quick release. The first method used in the glass box can be applied to the crystal casket also. A loose brass binding, held with bolts that fit in holes draw back to slots, will serve. These bolts are in the corners and are withdrawn by the assistants while moving the casket. This is not the ideal arrangement, first, because there is no excuse for delay and second, because the casket is very heavy and cannot well be moved. The curtains are placed around it or a cabinet lowered over it.

So Houdini planned a special release for the interior, and while his diagrams are lacking in mechanical details, they at least give the fundamental idea of the method he devised. There are hidden catches in the center of each portion of brass framework. The framework is enlarged at these points, because it connects with the hole in the center of the top. The diagrams indicate a single release for each of these catches, operating from the center of the top. This appears to be a twist of the center rim, giving a corresponding turn to the flat rods extending to the brass framework. The rods operating thus are the ones beneath the glass. One arrangement would be for this to turn or operate by moving the cap itself, and it is possible to have the turning take place only when the cap is in position; it is simpler, however, to have everything take place from beneath, in which case the rods can move independently, each being operated individually from a position at the center. Their release may also depend on pressure from pins used to set the cap in place.

These details, while based on a study of Houdini's sketches, are speculative; the important point is that he regarded such a release as being not only practical but also undetectable and preferable to any other. If his plans had proved unsatisfactory, the release used in the glass box could have been applied to the crystal casket also.

There are three factors in addition to its mechanical perfection that guard the secret of the release. First, there is much to be done and inspection is sure to be brief; second, everyone looks for trickery at the spot where the cover joins the casket, so that attention is centered there; third, the straps seem to preclude all possibility of any mechanical arrangement. It is these straps which are our next consideration. Having released the top of the cover, what can the performer do? These straps are not faked, and he is still in the cabinet.

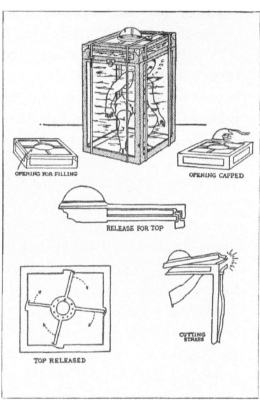

The brass binding offers the solution. It is not wide except at the corners and at the middle points where it joins with the strips or rods that go to the center of the top. In those spots it is apparently fastened to the woodwork, but the bolts are fakes or short bolts that fit in slots in the wood. Between the middle points and the corners, the binding does not come far below the glass. Now the straps will give, no matter how tightly they are fastened. They will not yield sufficiently to be of any use at the bottom

Fig. 47. *Details of the crystal water casket.*

of the cover, where the overhanging edge is thick and deep to make the casket entirely watertight; but at the binding only a little stretching is necessary to enable the performer to insert a thin-bladed knife between the binding and the woodwork. The straps pass by spots where the binding is not deep, and the knife can be worked through when the performer presses upward on the top of the cover.

Thus he cuts all four straps; then he lifts the top of the cover and leaves the box. There is one important point, however, which must not be overlooked. The performer has released the top; he has cut the straps; but what has he done for air in the meantime? He certainly cannot count on finishing operations on the straps before he is out of breath. The answer to this problem is found in the hemispherical cover that fits over the center of the top. It contains air; and when the performer needs a fresh supply, he goes back to it. The cap is smaller than his head; hence its purpose is not suspected. The performer gets the air by tilting his head backward so that his nose and mouth come out of the water!

Houdini evidently estimated that the few breaths the performer would require were contained within the cap, but he also had an emergency measure in case the cap should prove too small for its required purpose: the bottom of the cap was slightly faulty, so that when it was clamped down it could never lie absolutely flat on the rim beneath. As a result, the cap would not be airtight, and the performer's air supply could last almost indefinitely.

Once out of the casket, the performer's task is to remove the cut straps and replace them with duplicates hidden in the cabinet covering the casket. He must also replace the catches so that the top of the cover will be firmly in position.

That is why a tum of the cap is desirable, for the catches can then be thrown back from the outside of the casket. If such a mechanism is too complicated and the catches must be handled from inside the cover, the performer must unlock the locks, remove the cover, and fit the top portion into position. The locks, while genuine, are part of the casket, so that duplicate keys are easily retained by the performer. No water will come from the casket when the top is removed, for the performer's body has displaced a considerable quantity, and the level will normally be below the upper edge of the casket. If the glass box type of release is used (i.e., a release from outside the cabinet), the performer's task is simplified, as he has merely to undo the simple action of his assistants before the escape.

To the audience the crystal water casket is a sensational escape in which the odds are so greatly against the performer that his act of freeing himself seems miraculous. To the performer it is a workable device that requires nerve and ability but is well worth it because of its effectiveness. Houdini, with his fearlessness and strength, his ability and experience, could attempt escapes of this caliber and present them successfully where others would have hesitated and eventually abandoned the idea.

The Water Torture Cell

THE GREATEST AND MOST SENSATIONAL of all Houdini's escapes was without doubt his "Chinese Water Torture Cell" which, even from the experimental and blueprint period, was destined to become the biggest ever. It was, in a sense, a "double challenge"—first, to the audience, to solve it if they could, but never did; second, to his imitators to try to come up with something even half as wonderful.

How well Houdini succeeded in that latter purpose, the record itself shows. During his lifetime and for many years after, he was the only man to perform the escape from the Water Torture Cell, or anything quite like it, though it was not his skill and nerve alone that served him in such stead, as will be seen. Yet with all its seeming danger, and the definite difficulties which it presented, Houdini never failed in the escape.

That point must be specially stressed, because in the garbled version of Houdini's life that was produced as a feature movie, the script had him drowning in an outlandish contraption that looked like a prop man's dream and was every bit as intellectually unstimulating as the story itself. So, many years after Houdini's death, small-minded imitators had their "gloat" when the public was fed the false notion that Houdini had failed in an escape which they, the imitators, would never have attempted. In fact, few would have had the nerve to go into the cell as Houdini did, let alone try to get out of it.

The Chinese Water Torture Cell was definitely an evolution that incorporated features from many of Houdini's earlier escapes. To trace its development chronologically would be futile, as—like the Torture Cell itself—it had its ups and downs all along the line.

Fig. 48. *Houdini suspended over cell.*

In short, Houdini had some such creation in mind almost from the day when he began introducing special challenges and mechanical problems into his act. Every now and then he would come up with some intriguing device, thinking that he had found the ultimate, only to drop it and go back to earlier ideas.

Yet in the actual ultimate, as the Water Torture Cell became, we see the fruits of all these labors and more. That in itself is enough to rank it as Houdini's greatest escape. It should be added that the Water Torture Cell, or the "Upside Down" escape as Houdini termed it, also underwent a series of improvements that led to the construction of different cells, but these were nearly enough alike to be classed as about the same.

As far as the public was concerned, they *were* the same, for during the fiteen years that Houdini presented the Upside Down more or less continuously, the cell remained unchanged to the casual eye. Only the magical-minded observer would have noted the differences and even then it was necessary to see the act often, over a long period.

The genesis of the Water Torture Cell can be traced to two escapes: The Glass Box and the Milk Can. When placed inside the Glass Box, Houdini could be seen there before the cabinet was placed about it. This was a very effective feature for it quashed the motion that in some way Houdini might be "gone" before the escape even began.

In the Milk Can, the fact that Houdini was immersed in water was the striking feature, but the early posters and drawings of the milk can show it in cutout diagram form to illustrate what it was like inside. So eager was Houdini to give his audience an actual view of himself within the milk can that he planned a special "Glass Milk Can" for that very purpose. That idea gave way to such intriguing notions as the "Rubber Bag and Glass Box" and the "Crystal Water Casket." But in the meantime Houdini was working on his first Upside Down idea, that of being confined in a milk can which was to be inverted and put into a larger container from which he would also have to escape.

So the term "Upside Down," or the "USD" as Houdini sometimes abbreviated it, referred to certain escape devices planned or used by Houdini prior to the Chinese Water Torture Cell. But when that great masterpiece was finally unveiled, it took the title and became the only "USD" from that time on.

These points have been mentioned in order to establish some important facts regarding the Water Torture Cell, which was first exploited successfully as the principal feature of the Houdini show in Germany in the fall of 1912. This has been overlooked in some Houdini biographies,

Fig. 49. *Theo Hardeen (brother of Houdini) and Sidney Radner standing beside Houdini's Water Torture Cell. The grille has been removed from the cell.*

which set the date of the Water Torture Cell debut a full year or more later.

But by then, the Upside Down had already been hailed as one of Houdini's greatest escapes and since British magical journals of the period were replete with praise for the new mystery, the best way to set the record straight is to quote directly from them.

An early note in the *Magic Wand,* July 1911, is particularly significant, for it shows Houdini's concern in protecting his invention:

> Always on the lookout for something new and fresh, Houdini has recently perfected an extraordinary contraption which looks like a fish tank. This is filled with water, and H. is placed head down in it in full view of the audience. His feet are manacled in a variant of the old fashioned stocks, and when the tank is covered it is difficult to imagine how he can possibly escape. But escape he does ...

> Houdini is like most inventors and creators in that he suffers by reason of the attention of plagiarists. He tried patenting some of his earlier mystery contrivances, but he was not satisfied that this afforded him any real protection. He has now hit on a novel method which he hopes will euchre the attentions of his imitators, and it certainly would be to the benefit of magic if he does. He has registered this latest invention with the Lord Chamberlain as a play. He gave a special performance of it a short time ago to an audience of one man—a man who paid a guinea for a seat in the pit.

In the *Magician Monthly* for October 1912 we read:

> Harry Houdini is appearing at the Circus Busch, Berlin ... During his present engagement he has

broken all his previous records in that country. The Circus Busch is packed at every performance and his act is the talk of Berlin. He is featuring an "upside down" escape of an extraordinary character. Doubtless we shall presently see it in this country. For Houdini is booked to appear in London and some of the big provincial towns after his German season.

In the next issue, November 1912, there was reference to the fact that "Harry Houdini is finishing his continental tour and in the course of a week or two will be among us with his latest and most sensational escapes."

This comment was followed by the truly prophetic announcement in the December 1912 issue:

Harry Houdini has finished his continental tour and is now in England. He is booked for a series of engagements in this country and will shortly open in London. His program will be of a startling character. It will include mysteries more extraordinary than even he has yet presented to the public. His previous tours in this country have all been of a sensational character. We prophesy however—and we speak from knowledge of his proposed programme—that this one will eclipse in that respect all its predecessors.

The same magazine in its next issue, January 1913, came out in a big way regarding Houdini's new creation, with the announcement:

We have just received from our Cardiff correspondent an account of Houdini's appearance there... The public interest he aroused in Cardiff appears to have been quite exceptional. "Standing Room Only" was the rule at every performance; and crowds assembled in the streets to cheer him as he arrived at and left the theatre.

His great act was "The Water Torture Cell." The cell is filled with water; Houdini is placed in it head downwards; his ankles are clamped and locked above in the center of a massive cover. Yet he manages to escape! The act will doubtless make a great sensation in London, where Houdini will, we understand, appear at the end of next month.

To this was appended the comment that "Our artist, Mr. H. K. Elcock, contributes a brilliant cartoon of the great escape artiste to this number." The cartoon in question, while somewhat allegorical, did give a fairly good depiction of the Water Torture Cell.

Five months later, in the June 1913 issue, Elcock did even better when he sketched Houdini's entire act, showing each step of the Water Torture Cell in detail and including the Needle Trick, which was the other "extraordinary mystery" featured in Houdini's program.

Fig. 50. *H. K. Elcock's cartoon for* The Magician Monthly.

The *Magical World* of June 4, 1913 gave an equally graphic review of the Upside Down, which is practically a running commentary to Elcock's sketches. Here, according to that account, is how the act appeared at the New Cross Empire:

> In his present programme, Houdini is featuring a sensational escape from what is termed a "Water Torture Cell," a formidable appliance entirely of his own design and construction.
>
> He devotes about five minutes of the opening of his act to a detailed description of the tank, stocks, grill and steel tackle comprising the apparatus. The tank is of solid construction in mahogany, with the front panel of plate glass an inch in thickness.
>
> The top, or lid, is made in the form of the old fashioned stocks with holes provided for the reception of the ankles. The two halves are heavily hinged and provided with a strong snap-lock to secure the feet when encased. An outer frame of solid, angular steel is fitted to effectually prevent possible movement when once it encloses the wooden stocks.
>
> A metal cell, about the height and breadth of the performer, with a fronting grill of open metal bars, fits within the water tank, ostensibly to prevent the "victim" rising from his inverted position when once fixed in it. Bands of steel arranged in massive frets, hinged and padlocked, to envelop every side of the tank, complete the outfit.

Inviting a representative committee of the audience—about twelve—to minutely inspect the properties... Houdini retires for a moment or two to change while his active attendants rapidly fill the tank from a high-pressure hose and with buckets of heated water from ornamental cauldrons at either side of the setting.

Returning in swimming costume, Houdini lays on his back in the center of the stage as members of the committee adjust his feet within the stocks and snap the locks. The steel frame is next passed over the body until at the base of the stocks where it is clamped securely. The metal grill has been placed in the tank and pulleys haul the intrepid artiste in mid-air, where he remains suspended by his feet ready for his plunge into the water below.

A few seconds later he drops head foremost into the tank; the stocks are instantly fixed in place of a lid, the steel frets quickly cover the sides and top, leaving space in their design to give view of the performer's submerged head; locks are bustled on, and a handsome cabinet of draperies veil the rest.

Something like a thrill passes over the crowded theatre during the two minutes of suspense that follow. An axe, ready to break the glass in case of danger, attracts many an anxious eye. The orchestra with "Asleep in the Deep" helps to awaken the awful possibility of failure. But a second later, Houdini bursts his cabinet

and stands smiling and free to receive the enthusi-
astic plaudits of a bewildered house.

This was not the only review of Houdini's most sensational escape. A writer in the *Magician Monthly* covered
much of the same and added a few impressions that he
gained as a committee man during Houdini's performance
at the Finsbury Park Empire. He stated in regard to the
Water Torture Cell:

> The construction of it is so simple that the merest
> child in the audience can understand it. Each part is
> shown separately. The glass front is explained. It is
> necessary because of the danger of a mishap during
> the "escape." Houdini might faint or his nerve might
> suddenly give out. Is he to drown, then, to make a
> Finsbury Park Empire holiday? No; the watching
> assistant would smash the glass and the life of the
> great magician would be saved.

In later performances of the Water Torture Cell, Houdini
stressed that the steel "grille" or "cage," which was lowered
into the cell, also served as a safety measure, as well as
constituting another barrier against his escape. Houdini
told his audiences that if the glass were broken, either accidentally or in case of emergency, the bars of the cage would
prevent him from being carried into the jagged edges of the
glass when the water gushed out.

That was quite true, for bars were inside the glass. In
the earlier version of the Water Torture Cell, the bars were
horizontal; later, they were arranged vertically. There were
two plugs at the bottom of the cell to let the water out, both
as a safety measure and in order to empty it after each show.

If Houdini had really been trapped inside the cell, opening the two and three quarter inch diameter plugs might have been of considerable help.

It has already been mentioned that up to recent years Houdini was the only man who ever attempted an escape from the Water Torture Cell, or a device closely resembling it. But the act was closely imitated, perhaps actually duplicated, within a few months after Houdini introduced it; not by a man, but by a woman!

How Houdini met that challenge is a now little known story of show business and might be all-but-forgotten except for its passing mention in the columns of the *Magical World* and the survival of a unique playbill that substantiates the account. The same issue of the *Magical World* that reviewed the original Water Torture Cell contained this mention:

> "Miss Houdini" was advertised at the Theatre Aquarium, Moscow, last month, in her sensational water escape. But we fancy Harry Houdini knows something of this.

Harry Houdini knew a lot concerning it. The act in question was not originally billed as "Miss Houdini" as reported, but under the name of Miss Undina, which was about as close as the pirates could come to taking Houdini's name along with the invention that they actually pilfered. The whole story, and what Houdini did about it, was reported in the *Magical World* a few months later:

> While playing Circus Busch in Berlin last autumn, Houdini produced his new Water Torture Cell Illusion ... Two impresarios visited the circus repeatedly and assisted on the committee which Houdini

always invited into the ring or upon the stage to thoroughly examine his apparatus.

They are said to have been too thorough and to have measured the various parts as well. It is claimed that being well acquainted with certain employees of the circus, they also managed to gain access to Houdini's dressing room to inspect the stocks.

Later, while still performing at the circus, Houdini's attention was drawn to an advertisement in one of the professional papers illustrating a lady calling herself "Miss Undina" doing an exact copy of his new sensational act. Her lithographs were also obvious copies of his own.

Immediately, taking legal advice, Houdini instituted action and within a few days obtained an injunction which ordered the defendants not to produce or perform the act publicly, not to use similar lithographs, nor to claim publicly that they or Miss Undina were the "creators" of the act in question.

Fig. 51. *German poster advertising Undina.*

The injunction was followed by a further lawsuit wherein the court made the injunction permanent and ordered costs against the defendants.

Probably the "Miss Houdini" who appeared in Moscow was the "Miss Undina" from Berlin, rapidly heading off into obscurity, as the only tangible relic we have seen of her existence is an undestroyed lithograph that was used as an exhibit in the court case. As for the "water cell" from which she escaped, its greatest mystery is what finally became of it.

Houdini continued to present the one and original Chinese Water Torture Cell from that time on. It appeared that the ultimate in escapes had indeed been achieved. When Houdini did the Upside Down in England, in 1913, it literally "stopped the show" no matter what other acts were on the bill.

When he did the same escape in America in 1926, the year he died, it still stopped the show; but this time it was all his own show—a "full evening." With all the magic that he presented, all his skill at sleight of hand, all the spirit tricks he demonstrated, the Water Torture Cell still held the audience breathless and spellbound, during those two minutes and one second from the time the cabinet closed until Houdini reappeared free.

Here is how the greatest of all escapes, the amazing Upside Down was advertised in the New York World of June 1, 1913, as the great attraction then heading the bill at Hammerstein's:

HOUDINI

THE WORLD-FAMOUS SELF-LIBERATOR
PRESENTING THE GREATEST PERFORMANCE
OF HIS STRENUOUS CAREER, LIBERATING
HIMSELF AFTER BEING LOCKED IN THE
WATER TORTURE CELL (Houdini's own inven-
tion) WHILST STANDING ON HIS HEAD, HIS
ANKLES CLAMPED AND LOCKED IN THE
CENTER OF THE MASSIVE COVER—A FEAT
WHICH BORDERS ON THE SUPERNATURAL

$ 1,000 .00—Houdini offers this sum to anyone
proving that it is possible to obtain air in the
upside-down position in which he releases himself
from this WATER-FILLED TORTURE CELL

That offer was to stand for the next thirteen years, and
it could still be made today if he had lived. But the rather
surprising thing is that even before Houdini staged his
great triumph, the secret of the escape was really known.
This simply proves again that showmanship—as with the
Needle Trick—is the thing that really counts in the mystification of an audience.

With the Upside Down, which he finally constructed in
England and programed for the fall opening at the Circus
Busch, Houdini risked a small fortune on three factors:

First, that this was a creation which he could definitely
claim as his own, nothing closely resembling it ever having
been seen or worked before.

Second, that the cost of construction, both of the cell and
its special parts, plus the expense of transporting such an
apparatus, would discourage imitators.

Third, that no such imitator would be able to undergo the upside-down ordeal under water and at the same time be supple enough to effect an escape which required the ability of a contortionist.

Oddly, Houdini won out on the first count only, the one which he regarded as the least important. In his appearances in England and at the Circus Busch, he established a certain claim. Other countries offered less protection for original performers.

The second count was immediately nullified by the tremendous sensation which the Water Torture Cell produced. It so captured the public mind that expense meant nothing to would be imitators who were on the scene. So Houdini's present success threatened to be the undoing of his future. His rivals spent money freely to get the secret and duplicate the job.

That left the third "out," and they found a way around that, too, one so ingenious that Houdini himself had probably never given it a second thought. True, Houdini was the only man known to be in the business who could twist his way to an escape from such a contrivance. But a skilled contortionist—and especially a small woman of lithe build—could manage that part quite readily. So the opposition chose such a performer.

It was Houdini's cardinal rule, with all dangerous escapes and especially those of the underwater variety, to make sure that the device used was sure and efficient; and consistently so. It had to be, for him to work the escape successfully, night after night, show after show.

The long wake of imitators who met death or near disaster by relying on untested methods or intricate devices that eventually failed them, proved both the value and necessity of Houdini's policy.

The mere fact that he took emergency precautions, such as having an assistant ready with an ax, was not sufficient. This was something that even competent reviewers overlooked.

One observer, commenting on the Water Torture Cell and what would happen if Collins had to rush in and smash the glass to save Houdini's life, declared: "For once and for the first time, Houdini would have failed 'to make good.' But the defeat would not be final. The next evening would see another attempt which would surely be crowned with success."

That guess was only half right. If Houdini had failed, we believe he wouldn't have tried again. It would have been more like him to junk the apparatus, or put it in storage for a long time, or even give up the escape business entirely. With certain types of challenges, Houdini could have afforded a stalemate because they were supposed to be "impossible" escapes that no one had ever made; and therefore would be entitled to another try. But with an escape of Houdini's own invention, involving a Milk Can, Water Torture Cell, or any contrivance of such special construction, his prospective escapes were advertised and therefore guaranteed. Failure was the risk accepted by imitators; not by Houdini.

A study of the various underwater escapes that Houdini planned and tested during the evolution from the Milk Can to the Upside Down, shows that he considered types of mechanism that became more intricate as he proceeded, and therefore were correspondingly useless. In finally constructing the Water Torture Cell, Houdini had a mental flashback that was in itself an inspiration.

He switched from all suggested underwater gadgets to a totally different device, one which was definitely tried and true, the Pillory Escape. He couldn't do a "pillory" under water, so he hit on the ingenious idea of doing it above water, in the form of an escape from a pair of stocks.

Note carefully the wording of Hammerstein's advertisement, stating that Houdini would be "locked in" the cell while "standing on his head" which was true in a sense, but did not stress that he was actually locked in stocks which were set on the cell and attached to it.

Mention that his ankles were "clamped and locked" in the "massive cover" sounded as though this took place inside the cell proper. Again, there was no mention of stocks, as such.

The $1,000 reward was neatly worded, too. It gave the idea that Houdini was sealed inside a cell totally filled with water. Actually, there was a lot of air at the top, because water gushed in waves Over the brim when Houdini was let down quickly into the cabinet, and there was some leakage at joints. What apparently sealed the cell were Houdini's own ankles. The stocks and the edges of the top could not be labeled strictly airtight, but the reward specified that Houdini could not obtain air "in the upside-down position," which was true enough.

It was simply saying in other words that you can't get air when your head is 5 feet under water. From a magician's standpoint, the newspaper ad was extremely well worded, almost a masterpiece of misdirection itself, the way it stressed the "effect" and diverted attention from "method."

But in the German lawsuit, which preceded this, as well as the reviews, the stocks were emphasized. Elcock's sketches show Houdini's ankles being locked into them, and how he was lowered into the cell. Also stressed is Houdini's supposed inability to turn around, once encased in the cell and submerged there, the term "turn around" being interpreted to mean that he could not bring his head up to the top of the cell.

Actually, that was where Houdini's acrobatic ability served him well. Whether he could somersault himself forward in the grilled inner cage was a question; but there seems to be no doubt that he could do so in a sideward fashion in line of the diagonal. The inside cross section of one cell without snug-fitting grill-shell, was twenty-two by twenty-five inches, so the job could be measured in a diagonal, not width or depth; and however tight the squeeze for Houdini, there would be room to spare for a slender, short girl who was not necessarily a contortionist.

Fig. 52. *German poster advertising "The world renowned Houdini in his original invention."*

In either case, however, the feet had to be free for the performer to twist about at all. A release could be gained surely and swiftly with a sliding section like that used in a pillory escape. A pair of stocks matching the neck and wrist frames of the pillory would serve the ankles just as well, but with a downward rather than an upward slide.

An interesting feature of the Water Torture Cell is that the hinged stocks were actually incorporated into a solid, deep-set top, or to put it another way, Houdini, while experimenting with a conventional top, decided to convert it into a pair of stocks. This automatically eliminated all the complicated mechanical devices required in earlier types of water cells.

So the Water Torture Cell had an actual top that not only imprisoned Houdini but kept him in an upside-down position while the locks were being secured and the curtains were being closed. Yet all this was accomplished with rapid precision in a minimum amount of time, allowing that much more for the escape. In a late version, four hasps held the top framework; keys were inserted in each keyhole, locking the hasps, but secretly releasing the two boards which formed the stocks. The bars at the front of the cell enabled Houdini to gain a firm grip and work his body upward to apply full strength in getting his feet free. He could then twist sideways, draw his feet down into the cell, do a quick flip turnover and come up for air, head first.

The top was deep-set, like a box lid, its lower edges being bound with a metal frame. Houdini had no trouble getting his head above water level, which had already been lowered by the splash from his upside-down immersion. It was then a matter of opening the top "doors" fully and climbing out between the two stock boards that had been unlatched when the hasp-lock keys were turned. The two stock boards could then be slid open, drawer fashion. In an alternative device, they could be flipped open on end hinges. Houdini then let himself down outside the tank, closed it completely and made his dramatic appearance from the cabinet.

Oddly, the Water Torture Cell had one weakness when originally shown—the crossbars inside the front. They looked too much like a ladder, giving the impression that Houdini was not so helpless as he looked, because all he had to do was use the bars for rungs and walk up them.

That gave rise to theories of intricate devices like inside posts that Houdini could push up and thus work his way to freedom. All anyone had to do was see the Water Torture Cell performed a few times to recognize how ridiculous these "explanations" were. For example, to move the top of the Cell requires at least two men. Not only would Houdini have needed to push up more than his own weight, the outer cabinet would have had to be twice as high as the Torture Cell, though actually it had only a few feet headway.

Nor did any of these know-alls allow for the release from the stocks. Houdini would still have been hanging from them, out of water instead of in it, but unable to free himself further.

With many stage illusions, such crackpot explanations were often to be encouraged as they drew attention from the real secret. But Houdini's Water Torture Cell was supposed to be more than an illusion. It had to be an impossibility that "bordered on the supernatural" as the press notices claimed. So the bars were later changed and placed verti-cally instead of horizontally. They no longer looked like the rungs of a ladder, so no one thought in those terms.

How close some observers came to the acceptance of a "supernatural" theory where Houdini's underwater escapes were concerned, is evidenced by this quotation from the fifth edition of *Spirit Intercourse: Its Theory and Practice,* by J. Hewat McKenzie, a firm believer:

> The author saw Houdini demonstrate his powers of dematerialization before thousands, upon the public stage of the Grand Theatre, Islington, London. Here a small iron tank, filled with water, was deposited upon the stage, and in it Houdini was placed, the water completely covering his body ...
>
> Without disturbing any of the locks, Houdini was transferred from the tank direct to the back of the stage in a dematerialized state. He was there materialized and returned to the stage front dripping with water ...
>
> While the author stood adjacent to the tank during the dematerialization process, a great loss of physical energy was felt by him, such as is usually experienced by sitters in materializing seances, who have a good stock of vital energy, as in such phenomena a large amount of energy is required ...
>
> Not only was Houdini's body dematerialized, but it was carried through the locked iron tank, thus demonstrating the passage of matter through matter. This startling manifestation of one of nature's

profoundest miracles was probably regarded by most of the audience as a clever trick.

Mr. McKenzie evidently referred to Houdini's Milk Can Escape rather than the Water Torture Cell, but as his book appeared after Houdini had begun to do the Torture Cell, most believers accepted it as the "dematerialization" demonstration, particularly as it was the only underwater escape that Houdini presented on the stage from then on.

Up until Houdini's death, all during the time that he was denouncing fraud mediums and exposing their trickery, believers

Houdini's

SCENE AND PROP. LIST

Open and close in full stage. (Palace.)

Time of act—About 25 minutes.

As I leave stage soaking wet in bathing suit, require two dressing rooms nearest stage (6 in company). Couch in dressing room.

Require a small trap in center of stage, not less than 8 inches square (8x8 inches) two feet in rear of front cloth.

Must have use of Fire Hose to reach from side of stage, about 3 feet past center of stage. Hose is used in view of audience.

Please see to it that the water in Hose is run off. It must be clear, so that audience can see through same.

100 gallons of Boiling water (must be boiling).

We carry four brass tubs to hold this water, which must be filled ready on stage before each performance.

Prepare a chute, or get-away, for 250 gallons of water, from the small 8x8-inch trap to most convenient spot underneath stage. The outlet in our Water Cloth is 6 inches in Diameter .

Our Water Carpet must be tied after each show back of stage, for which we require a strong batten.

Two small occasional tables (gold if possible, and 4 gold chairs) and 18 Bent-wood Chairs.

A run or stair case, so that committee from audience can come over footlights onto stage.

A small, clean looking (mahogany colored if possible) step ladder about 3 feet 6 inches high.

Two 20 feet and two 16 feet lengths of Lumber 4 inches by 2 inches (4x2 inches), or battens would do, which must be 4 inches wide.

PLEASE DO NOT PURCHASE ANYTHING AT MY EXPENSE

Fig. 53

insisted that Houdini actually dematerialized himself from the water cell. They argued that he was afraid to admit his mediumistic powers in the face of public antagonism.

Yet oddly, gullible believers in the psychic are no more blind than some of the inventive skeptics who claim that they know every trick and that none are any good unless they originated them. One master magical mechanic made the comment regarding Houdini's Water Torture Cell:

When the big cabinet is closed around the tank, anyone interested enough to think about it at all, easily supposes that men come up through the floor and let him out. In fact, that is the way the trick should be done. Why not?

The question "Why not?" is easily answered by anyone who saw Houdini present the Water Torture Cell. In his earliest performances of the escape, he insisted that the committee examine the stage and offered to move the cell to any spot they wanted. Not only that, because of the heavy overflow during the filling of the tank and Houdini's immersion later, a canvas tarp was spread and the tank set on it, as was done with the Milk Can Escape.

Believers in the occult and avowed skeptics had something very much in common where Houdini was concerned: they could both be 100 percent wrong in explaining how he accomplished his most spectacular escapes.

About Houdini

THE LIFE STORY of Houdini is a simple one. This may surprise those who have tried to weave a touch of mysticism into his career, or credit him with the possession of supernormal power. There was no mumbo jumbo about Houdini in any form whatever.

From boyhood, Houdini was driven by a double-barreled ambition to achieve success in the field he cherished most. This ideal was Americanism; not occultism. The field he happened to like was magic; not in the sense of the necromancer, or pretender to the supernatural; but that of the conjurer, or prestidigitator.

But Houdini didn't think in those terms at the start. Perhaps the best way to gain an inkling as to his real thoughts is to read his own story as he told it in some autobiographical notes which appeared after he had solidly established the fame which he had suddenly achieved, yet still had greater goals ahead.

Here was what Houdini, wrote:

> My birth occurred April 6, 1874, in the small town of Appleton, Wisconsin. My father, the Rev. Dr. Mayer Samuel Weiss, at that time received an annual

salary of $750. Some of the leading factors in the congregation, thinking he had grown too old to hold his position, supplanted him for a younger man.

One morning my father awoke to find himself thrown upon the world, his long locks of hair having silvered in service, with seven children to feed, without a position, and without any visible means of support. We thereon moved to Milwaukee, where such hardships and hunger became our lot that the less said on the subject, the better.

October 28, 1883 was the date of my first appearance before an audience. I appeared as a contortionist and trapeze performer, being advertised by the manager, Jack Hoeffler, as "Ehrich, The Prince of the Air."

That was the first time that the future Houdini worked under the name of "Erich"—which was his own; though later he shortened it to "Eric the Great." His family wanted him to stay at home, which he did for a time, only to go with the circus at intervals, hoping to make more money than he could at prosaic jobs.

As Houdini continued, in his story:

Later in life, I worked at a number of trades, such as locksmith, electrical driller, photographer, cutter, etc., etc.; but I prefer to pass rapidly by those hard and cruel years when I rarely had the bare necessities of life and speak of the time when I first started to do handcuff tricks—the tricks that eventually brought me to the notice of the world.

One day while working as an apprentice in a lock-smith's shop close by the police station, one of the young bloods of the town was arrested for some trivial offence. He tried to open his handcuffs with some keys he had on his person; and in the attempt broke off one of the keys in the lock of the handcuff. He was brought to the shop to have the cuff opened or cut off his wrist, and this incident, trivial as it may seem, in after years changed my entire career.

While the master locksmith was trying to open the handcuff the whistle blew the dinner hour. Having a sharpened appetite, he called me to his side and said, "Harry, get a hack-saw and cut off this hand-cuff," and then went out with the police officer to dine. I tried to cut off the cuff, but the steel was too hard, and after breaking half-a-dozen saw blades, the thought struck me to attempt to pick the lock. I succeeded in doing it, and the very manner in which I then picked the lock of the handcuff contained the basic principle which I employed in opening hand-cuffs all over the world. Not with a duplicate key, which seems to have been the only way others had of duplicating my performance.

That was the only incident that Houdini mentioned in the years that he "preferred to pass by"; but his friend of many years, Joseph Rinn, has provided some data in between. In 1889 Rinn met the young Houdini at the Pastime Athletic Club in New York and learned that he was interested in magic, which was also Rinn's hobby.

With Houdini, however, it was a serious matter. He was doing shows with a partner, Jack Hayman, who worked in the same shop, and between times he was reading the memoirs of Robert-Houdin, the famous French magician of a generation before. One day Erich Weiss told Joseph Rinn: "I've made up my mind, Joe, to quit my job and become a professional magician under the name of Harry Houdini."

He took the name "Houdini" because it signified "Like Houdin," who was then his idol. In the fall of 1891, Harry persuaded his partner, Jack Hayman, to go along with him as the "Houdini Brothers," but it didn't work out. For a while Jack's brother Joe filled in as the junior member of the Houdini Brothers; then Harry took on his own brother, Theo.

Finally, in 1894, Harry married Beatrice Rahner, and they became "the Houdinis."

Fig. 54. *Houdini and his brother Theo Hardeen.*

They were billed as "Monsieur" and "Mademoiselle" Houdini, which indicated that the influence of the famous French wizard, Robert-Houdin, was still a prime factor in Houdini's career. But Houdini did not dwell on this in his brief autobiography. Instead, he went on to relate:

> The year 1893 found me an actor! I played the part of an old man in a play entitled "My Uncle" ... The show was such a success that the only way possible for me to get back to St. Louis was to deposit my trick trunk as security for railroad fares.
>
> It was while in St. Louis that I formulated the basis of my method for performing my packing-box escape and it happened in this wise: The winter was a bitterly cold one and I had no money with which to purchase wood to start a fire to warm my room. So seeing a discarded packing-case in front of one of the large dry-goods' shops, I thought I would take it home for firewood.
>
> I knew I would make myself too conspicuous by carrying so large a case through the streets and further knew that no police officer would permit me to break it apart in so crowded a thoroughfare, so I conceived a method of taking it noiselessly apart, and used this same method when I presented the packing-case mystery for the first time in Essen Ruhr, Germany ...

Houdini's friend, Rinn, commented on the fact that Houdini was working as a "single" act at the time mentioned above and also quotes from a playbill which the Houdinis issued in 1894, which stated:

NOTICE TO MANAGERS

A Startling Feature-Time of Act, 15 Minutes
Our Act Has Been Featured in:
Maskelyne & Cook's Egyptian Hall, London
Oxford-Cambridge
and
Robert Houdin's, Paris
We Will Forfeit $1000 if Any Detail of
Our Act Given Herewith Is Misrepresented
Harry and Bessie Houdini

If those "details" included where the Houdinis had played, not just the description of the act itself, they should have forfeited $1000 then and there, for they had never been abroad, let alone played a theater of any account. But as Rinn commented, Houdini couldn't have afforded to forfeit even $10 at that time. This was more than wishful thinking on Houdini's part. He was fictionizing the past as he pictured the future, a wonderful process for a youth who believed he had a date with destiny. But the Houdinis still couldn't get anything better than beer hall and dime museum showings, with the exception of a week in vaudeville at Tony Pastor's Theater, late in January 1895. So in the spring they went with a tent show, which was little more than a glorified carnival, judging from Houdini's own account, which continues:

In 1895, I was engaged by the Welsh Brothers' Circus which traveled almost exclusively through the State of Pennsylvania, and for the services of Mrs. Houdini and myself I received the sum of $20 weekly, railroad fares and board.[4]

The amount was small, but I still look back with pleasure upon that season's work as being one in which we had an abundance of clothes to wear and good food to eat, for the Welsh Brothers certainly fed their artists extra well.

For this $20 weekly, Mrs. Houdini and myself first of all had to give a free performance in front of the side show to attract the crowds. Inside, I then lectured upon the curiosities, gave a magic show, worked the Punch and Judy show, and with the assistance of Mrs. Houdini finally presented a second sight act. In the main concert, Mrs. Houdini acted as the singing clown, while later on we presented our specialty, which consisted of the trunk trick in connection with the braid trick. With this same performance, we later created a big sensation at the Alhambra Theatre in July 1900.

I offered my handcuff act to the Welsh Brothers for $5 extra per week, but it was rejected. Eventually, I offered to clown the bars, collect lithographs, and do my handcuff show for $3 extra per week, and it also was refused.

---

4 Mrs. Houdini's recollection was that they received $25, but she may have inadvertently included an extra $5 that Houdini wanted, but did not get.

In fact, several managers later on refused to allow me to do handcuffs, and it was only after persistently presenting it every once in a while like a trick in several museums, that I eventually was allowed to do the act steadily, and only after I had become known to the managers.

During 1895 the Houdinis toured with a show called "The American Gaiety Girls" and after it folded they joined a magician known as Marco, working as his assistants and doing their trunk trick in Nova Scotia and New Brunswick, in 1896. That show also went broke; but during that period, Houdini worked a few "challenge" escapes as publicity stunts, including a release from handcuffs supplied by the police.

He then went West, but found it difficult to obtain theatrical bookings. As Houdini himself told it:

In 1897, I appeared with a medicine show in the Indian Territory, with Drs. Hill and Pratt. I had to sell medicine on the streets from the carriage, and exhibited my prowess to the gaping public, free of charge. We received as salary $25 weekly, board and traveling expenses, and from this engagement we managed to save our first $100.

In 1898, things became so bad that I contemplated quitting the show business, and retiring to private life, meaning to work by day at one of my trades—being really proficient in several—and open a school of magic, which with entertainments would occupy my evenings. I therefore started to play one more tour of the Dime Museums to fulfill my expiring contracts, and it was this tour which made Houdini, the Handcuff King, famous.

When working at a small hall in St. Paul, a party of managers happened to come in. They saw my performance, became impressed with the manner in which I presented it, and one of them, Mr. Martin Beck, perhaps more in a joke than sincerity, challenged me to escape from one of his handcuffs. He had none with him, but next day purchased a few pairs and sent them on stage. I escaped! He then booked me for one week and it was the first chance I ever had, and my act in a first-class theater created a sensation. My salary for this week's engagement was $60. In those days I opened my performance with fifteen minutes of magic, but gradually dropped it out until handcuffs were exclusively presented in connection with the trunk trick.

From there on, it was unnecessary for Houdini to go into details of his theatrical career as it was written in playbills, headlines, and challenges. During his American vaudeville tour he shook off handcuffs and escaped from jails and was such a success that he gambled on a trip to Europe, in June 1900, and became an immediate sensation in England, his fame traveling with him to the Continent.

Here is an announcement that Houdini published:

$5,000 Reward for One Misstatement.

If this Record were Published as Fiction it would Not be Believed.

This June, 1901, **HOUDINI** has been in Europe one Year!

Arrived in London without one day's contract, and not even a promise. After several trial shows, and private exhibitions, was engaged for two weeks by the astute manager, Mr C. D. Slater, Alhambra, and stayed until the last week in August; it was impossible to stay longer as I had signed contracts for Germany with Mr. Slater's consent, but was re-engaged for the Holiday months to open December, making it the record for quick return engagements.

September, 1900.—Broke the record for paid admissions at the CENTRAL THEATRE, DRESDEN, Saxony. Management wires to Wintergarten to release Houdini, so he could stay another month. **But Wintergarten refuses.**

In the history of show business no act or feature has ever created the sensation or caused the talk in Berlin that Houdini caused month October, 1900. Wintergarten wires to Roanachers, Vienna, to allow Houdini to stay another month, Vienna is willing if London Alhambra will put Houdini's date one month forward. **Alhambra refuses.** Houdini proved such a draw that the Wintergarten pays a fine of 4,000 marks (about $1,000.00) to Vienna, so they could have him for month November.

Houdini opens at Magdeberg, Germany, for ten days. Management offers to pay Alhambra, London, two weeks salary fine to allow Houdini to stay two weeks longer. **Alambra refuses.**

Houdini opened re-engagement December 10th, played two months, making as big a hit as when he first opened.

Played one week for Mr Frank McNaughton, at Bradford People's Palace, packed them in to suffocation every show. Friday, Feb. 8th, 1901, drew such a crowd that **standing room was sold at 10 Shillings**, and hundreds failed to get in.

Drew crowded houses in Appollo Theatre, Dusseldorf, Crystal Palast, Leipzig; sold out houses **at raised prices** in Orpheum, Frankfort, A. M., and Hansa Theatre, Hamburg, Germany.

Booked for 10 days at Colosseum Essen a d Ruhr, prolonged 5 more, and again retained 15 more. Positively drew the biggest business and largest houses ever seen or heard of in Essen. People turned away every night, and last night all standing room was sold out at 8 marks each and stage was cleared and seats were sold where the scenery is supposed to stand. Management presents Houdini with a solid silver cup, 15 inches high and weighing 40 pounds, all inlaid with the 1900 issue of 3 and 5 mark pieces, there being over 600 marks in money on cup alone.

Drawing big salaries and big houses are not always mates, but Houdini has proven that as a drawing card he has no equal. Pretty fair for one year's work.

I heartily wish to thank Manager C. Dundas Slater for releasing me from my original contract, so that I could fill the German and Continental contracts.

Permanent address, Alhambra Theatre, London, England.

Fig. 55

During the profitable but strenuous years that followed, Houdini successfully accepted all sorts of challenges including an escape from a zinc-lined Russian prison van used to transport prisoners to Siberia. Houdini managed this, to the amazement of the Czar's police, by cutting his way through the bottom so neatly that the cut edges were not detected later.

When the police of Cologne, Germany, claimed that Houdini was misrepresenting his ability, he sued them for slander and won his case, proving his point by making an escape in open court, using a set of manacles with a special lock that the Cologne police had designed to thwart him!

In cities as far removed as Paris, France, and Melbourne, Australia, Houdini demonstrated his ability as a Handcuff King by leaping shackled into rivers and freeing himself while under water.

Whatever the challenge, Houdini took it on; and that was responsible for the coincidental link between the packing case that Houdini broke up for firewood in St. Louis and his escape in Essen Ruhr, Germany, years later.

As Houdini described it:

> The presentation of this mystery resulted from a challenge issued to me, more in jest than earnest, by one of the employees of a large linen factory which I visited while in that city. One of the men, packing a case of linens to send to America, recognized me and knowing I had just escaped from the local jail, laughingly said, "If we nail you in this packing case like we do linens, you would never be able to get out." Jokingly, I replied, "Oh, that would be easy," and proceeded on my way, thinking the incident was closed. Next day, on reading the morning newspaper, to my astonishment, I found that the packers had publicly challenged me to escape from one of their packing cases, into which they proposed to nail and rope me. My thoughts flew back to the year long gone by when I secured firewood to heat my room and I determined to accept their challenge, meaning to escape by using as a basis the method I had employed in securing my firewood years ago.
>
> It was a sensation and has been the means of putting a few solid stones in the foundation of my reputation.

*Fig. 56. Before the German
judiciary in Cologne, 1902.*

The "secret" of the Packing Box Escape was basically this: Houdini had found that the removal of a few nails made it possible to swivel one or more boards inward, providing a quick exit from the box. So he designed a special cutting tool, like a pair of thin pliers, which could be worked between the boards to cut the nails in question.

Often this could be done after the box was delivered to the theater, but when it was nailed together on the stage or kept constantly in sight of the challengers, Houdini would smuggle the cutter into the box with him and do the work himself. Later the cut nails would be pulled out and replaced by new ones, leaving the box intact. All this took place inside the cabinet, except when the box was used for an underwater escape instead of the handcuff leap. Then assistants reclaimed it afterward and replaced the nails. Houdini also had other boxes of much heavier construction, some with boards that screwed tightly in place and could not be loosened that easily. Some of these—including those designed for underwater escapes—are described elsewhere in this book.

Samples of Houdini's daring jumps and their attendant dangers are found in the following report:

Houdini's leap from the Frederichstrasse Bridge in Berlin, Germany, heavily manacled, September 5, 1908; his daring plunge into the Weser, Bremen, having to break the ice; Paris, from the roof of the gruesome Morgue, April 7, 1909, brought record houses, causing his imitators to try and duplicate his feats.

Two were fortunately saved from a watery grave: Alburtus, in Atlantic City, being saved by the life guards; Menkis was brought up in an unconscious state; and Ricardo jumped handcuffed from the Luippold Bridge, Landshut, Bavaria, April 14, 1909, and was drowned.

Cold waters have no terrors for Houdini, as in addition to the Weser leap, he dived manacled into the Mersey River, Liverpool, December 7, 1908, also into the Egbaston River, Birmingham, December 15, 1908. In all dives Houdini makes use of the regulation police handcuffs, chains and leg irons.

Houdini's autobiographical notes were made late in 1909, so we cannot work from his own chronological account following that time, though his diaries as well as news stories have enabled biographers to follow his career quite closely. The fact that he had by then become famous also contributed much data.

Fig. 57. *Houdini shackled for bridge jump.*
Mrs. Houdini is at the rear.

Many of his more important escapes and challenges are detailed and explained elsewhere in this book, so there is no need to list them here. In his engagement at Hammerstein's in the summer of 1912, he escaped from a straitjacket strapped on him by asylum attendants; from a locked milk can filled with water that was also locked inside an airtight case; from an operating table on which he was strapped by physicians; from a Sangwar Punishment Frame to which three Chinese roped and chained him; from soaked sheets in which he was wrapped by a committee of graduate nurses; from an export packing case; from a solid leather, copper-riveted punishment suit put on him by special sergeants of the U.S. Marine Corps.

It was at that time that Houdini first presented his "Submerged Box Feat" when he was lowered into New York Bay in the presence of a huge crowd, with iron weights lashed to the box. Whether or not Houdini was the first person to escape from an "overboard box" of one type or another, later became the subject of much controversy.

Fig. 58. *Houdini's bridge jump.*

With the formal introduction of his Chinese Water Torture Cell or Upside Down escape in the fall of 1912, Houdini rapidly eliminated most of his other and less spectacular escapes. He still did the Overboard Box, however, working that escape from the huge 250,000-gallon tank at the New York Hippodrome, while he was performing the Vanishing Elephant illusion on the same stage, in 1918.

After World War I, Houdini turned to motion pictures, appearing as the star in such "silent features" as "The Grim Game" and "Terror Island." In the early days of aviation, Houdini had taken an airplane with him to Australia and had become the first man to fly on that continent. So in "The Grim Game" he decided to do the daring feat of switching from one plane to another while in flight.

There was no fakery; Houdini never went in for that in any of his stunts. But the planes came so close that they collided and crashed to earth, fortunately without serious injury to Houdini or the other occupants. All this was actually filmed, however, so the script of "The Grim Game" was changed to include the first real plane crash ever recorded in pictures.

Houdini later produced his own feature films, "The Man From Beyond" and "Haldane of the Secret Service." By that time, in the early 1920s, a great wave of superstitious belief in pretended psychic phenomena was sweeping the country, encouraged by such noted persons as Sir Oliver Lodge and Sir Arthur Conan Doyle, who were convinced that such phenomena were real. So Houdini—a firm skeptic in such matters—went on a lecture tour exposing the "spirit frauds" which he had investigated.

He was still at this when he took out his full evening show in the fall of 1925 and the final act was an expose of the tricks used by fraudulent mediums. Again, Houdini dealt in challenges, but this time he was the challenger. Instead of inviting people to challenge him with intricate devices from which he guaranteed to escape on his own stage, he challenged so-called mediums to produce their raps, materializations, and other manifestations there.

None ever did, though on various occasions debates and other attempts were made to prove the existence of psychic phenomena by mediums who came to the theater where Houdini was playing. One such affair was held before a packed house on the evening of February 10, 1926, at the Chestnut Street Opera House in Philadelphia. No "spooks" were forthcoming, so Houdini emerged the complete victor.

Houdini followed that by a "return debate" a week or so later, this time on the stage of the Broad Street Theatre which the "opposition" hired for the occasion. Again, Houdini scored on every count. In June of the same year, Houdini made another trip to Philadelphia to challenge John Slater, known as the "Millionaire Medium," who was giving an exhibition of "sealed message reading" at Lu Lu Temple.

Accompanied by the same committee of judges who had been present on the two previous occasions, Houdini offered Slater a certified check for $10,000 if he could read any of three sealed messages that Houdini had brought with him. Slater did not even attempt to take up the offer.

On August 5, 1926 Houdini was "buried alive" in an airtight casket which was submerged in the swimming pool in the Hotel Shelton in New York for one hour and thirty-one minutes. He underwent this ordeal to spike the claims of an Egyptian fakir, Rahman Bey, who had been similarly confined for an hour and attributed it to a cataleptic trance. Houdini insisted that it could be done by simply breathing easily and conserving oxygen, and apparently he proved his point.

However, Houdini was ready for emergencies. He had a telephone to the casket connected by underwater cables and also an alarm bell with electric batteries that were in the casket itself, so that if one failed he could use the other to call for help.

Actually, the alarm bell wasn't needed and its batteries took up valuable air space. Houdini had it there in case *he* failed in the test; not the telephone. In that case, Houdini would have tried the test again, but the alarm bell "batteries"—already accepted as such—could well have contained a hidden supply of oxygen and carbon dioxide absorbent which Houdini could have used to prolong his underwater stay.

Houdini was ready to accept challenges to escape from underground as well as underwater. His escapes from locked safes and vaults had taught him well the value of conserving air, just as his ability to hold his breath helped him in his overboard escapes.

On that subject, Houdini himself stated:

> When I am nailed securely within a weighted packing case and thrown into the sea, or when I am buried alive under six feet of earth, it is necessary to preserve absolute serenity of spirit. I have to work with great delicacy and lightning speed. If I grow panicky, I am lost. If something goes wrong, if there is some little accident or mishap, some slight miscalculation, I am lost unless all my faculties are working on high, free from mental strain or tension. The public sees only the thrill of the accomplished trick. They have no conception of the tortuous preliminary self-training that was necessary to conquer fear.

Houdini took the airtight metal casket with him on his tour in the fall of 1926, so that he could repeat the test— underwater or underground—and outdo Rahman Bey or anyone else who managed to break his record.

In Detroit he collapsed from an advanced case of appendicitis, the result of a seemingly minor injury sustained a few days earlier. It was too late for an operation to save him, and he died on October 31, 1926—Halloween and now National Magic Day.

Houdini's body was brought back to New York in the metal casket in which he had undergone the submerged living burial in the water of the Shelton Pool. By a strange oddity of fate, it was the only box of any description that Houdini had entered, yet never escaped from, during life. Now, the same applied in death.

Fig. 59. *Houdini and Mrs. Houdini, Nice, 1913.*

Acknowledgements

The authors are indebted to The Library of Congress for numerous illustrations from the John J. and Hanna M. McManus and Morris N. and Chesley V. Young Collection, and the Harry Houdini Collection; also for the very special co-operation of Frederick R. Goff, Chief of the Rare Books Division. Additional institutional sources of reference material were the Theatre Collection of the New York Public Library and the Research Library of the New York Historical Society, both providing several photographs for use herein.

Also gratefully acknowledged is the unique assistance provided by Milbourne Christopher, Sidney Radner, and Larry Weeks, each prominent in his own way in the amassing of Houdiniana. Mr. Christopher of New York City, professional magician of world repute and magic historian, made much factual material available. Mr. Radner of Holyoke, Massachusetts, noted as a present-day escape artist and lecturer-demonstrator of fraudulent gambling practices, owns Houdini's Chinese Water Torture Cell, milk can, torture pillory, and many other pieces of equipment and memorabilia; opportunity was given to study these, and loan made of a hitherto unpublished photograph. Mr. Weeks of New York City, a juggler of high repute and also adept in escapes, is without doubt the outstanding collector of Houdini on motion picture film; he enabled us to observe Houdini in action in rare films and also loaned several photographs for use as illustrations.

Other illustrations are from one of the authors' (W.B.G.) personal collection.

Reminiscences of early Houdini days were personally provided by Lewis Goldstein, only living member of the Houdini show during the Handcuff Era of the early 1900s. Goldstein also worked with the Hardeen company during that same period, and the authors appreciate his first-hand recollections. From Douglas Geoffrey, successor to the Houdini-Hardeen show, the authors obtained valuable data pertaining to effects presented by Houdini in his full evening show, which was carried on by his brother Hardeen. Geoffrey, who appeared as Hardeen, Jr., in the road show of *Hellz-A-Poppin,* still performs some of the original illusions featured by Houdini.

The authors in full appreciation acknowledge the permission granted by Harcourt, Brace and Co. to reprint material from *Houdini's Escapes* by Walter B. Gibson, copyright 1930 by Bernard M. L. Ernst and from *Houdini's Magic* by Walter B. Gibson, copyright 1932 by Bernard M. L. Ernst.

Bibliography

(Including suggested additional reading)

ANONYMOUS: *Magic Made Easy.* New York, Wehman Bros., 1910.

CANNELL, J. C.: *The Secrets of Houdini.* London, Hutchinson & Co., Ltd., 1932.

DOYLE, SIR ARTHUR CONAN: *Our American Adventure.* London, 1923.

ENCYCLOPAEDIA BRITANN ICA: *Conjuring.* [11th edition] [Article signed: H.H .]

GIBSON, WALTER B.: *Houdini's Escapes.* New York, Harcourt, Brace and Co., 1930.

Houdini's Magic. New York, Harcourt, Brace, 1932.

and YOUNG, MORRIS N., Co-editors: *Houdini On Magic.* New York, Dover Publications, Inc., 1953.

GOLDSTON, WILL, Ed.: *Exclusive Magical Secrets.* London, 1912.

Further Exclusive Magical Secrets. London, 1927.

More Exclusive Magical Secrets. London, 1921.

Tricks and Illusions. London, 1908.

GRESHAM, WILLIAM LINDSAY: · *Houdini. The Man Who Walked Through Walls.* New York, Henry Holt, 1959.

HARDEEN, THEO.: *Life and History of Hardeen.* 20 Years of an Eventful Career on the Stage. Fully Illustrated, Containing Numerous Tricks and Secrets Especially Compiled by Hardeen.

HOFMANN, PROF. *[Pseud.* Lewis, Angelo John]: *Modern Magic.* London, 1876. [Reprinted in many editions, London and New York.]

More Magic. London, 1890. [Reprinted in many editions, London and New York.)

HOUDINI, HARRY: *Elliott's Last Legacy.* By Dr. James William Elliott. Edited by Harry Houdini. New York, Adams Press Print, 1923.

The adventurous Life of a Versatile Artiste. New York [190?] Rev. 1920 ed. New York, 1920.[Also other editions.]

A *Magician Among the Spirits.* New York, Harper & Bros., 1924.

Houdini's Paper Magic. New York. E. P. Dutton & Co., 1922.

Life, History and Handcuff Secrets of Houdini. [Several editions and printings.]

Magical Rope Ties and Escapes. London, Will Goldston, Ltd., 1921.

Mein Training; mein Tricks. Leipzig, 1909.

Miracle Mongers and Their Methods. New York, E. P. Dutton, 1920.

The Unmasking of Robert-Houdin. New York, 1908.

JARRETT, GUY: *Magic and Stage Craft*. New York [Aut.] 1936.

KELLOCK, HAROLD: *Houdini, His Life Story*. From the Recollections and Document of Beatrice Houdini. New York, Harcourt, Brace and Co., 1928.

McKENZIE, JAMES HEWAT: *Spirit Intercourse*. Its Theory and Practice. London, 1916; New York, 1917.

MYSTO MAGIC CO. [Alfred C. Gilbert]: Catalogue. New Haven, Conn., 1911.

OSGOOD, WHITMAN: *The Adventurous Life of a Versatile Artist*. Houdini. [Several editions and printings.]

RINN JOSEPH: *Sixty Years of Physical Research*. Houdini and I Among the Spiritualists. New York, The Truth Seeker Co., Inc., 1950.

SHAW, W.H.J.: New Ideas in Magic. St. Louis, 1902.

WILLIAMS, BERYL and EPSTEIN, SAMUEL: *The Great Houdini, Magician Extraordinary*. New York, Julian Messner Inc., 1950.

SERIALS CITED

Conjurers' Monthly Magazine, The. [Harry Houdini, ed. and contributing author.] New York, Vols. I and II, Sept. 1906 to Aug. 1908.

London [Eng.] *Daily Express*.

Magazine of Magic, The. [Goldston.] London.

Magic. [Edited by Ellis Stanyon.] London.

Magic Wand, The. [Edited by George MacKenzie Munro, and later, George Johnson.] London.

Magical World, The. [Ed. by Max Sterling.] Manchester, Eng.

Magician Annual, The. [Comp. and Ed. by Will Goldston.] London. 1907-11.

Magician Monthly, The. [Ed. by Will Goldston, and later, Bernard Irving.] London.

Mahatma. New York. 1895-1906.

World, The. New York, N.Y.

Pittsburgh [Penna.] *Sun.*

Sheffield [Eng.] *Independent.*

Sphinx, The. [Ed. by A. M. Wilson, and later, John Mulholland.] Kansas City, Mo.; New York, N.Y.

Wizard, The. [Selbit.] [Later continued as *The Magic Wand,* London.]

About the Authors

WALTER B. GIBSON is a professional writer and for many years, Houdini's amanuensis. Following Houdini's death, the attorney for the estate permitted him to examine much of Houdini's private scrapbooks and notes, from which Gibson wrote *Houdini's Magic* and *Houdini's Escapes* in the 1930's. These documents and others form the background for the present book. With Dr. Young, Mr. Gibson compiled and edited *Houdini on Magic*. He is the author of numerous books and articles on magic; and his prolific writing in the mystery fiction field includes *The Shadow* novels, which appeared in *The Shadow Magazine* under the pen name of Maxwell Grant, which continued over a period of fifteen years. He was also producer and narrator of Strange, a radio drama of the weird and supernatural, which was broadcast over a national network. In 1945, with Hardeen, Houdini's brother, Gibson revived the *Conjurer's Magazine,* founded by Houdini some forty years before. Gibson also toured with such noted magicians as Blackstone, Thurston and Raymond. His affiliations have included the Mystery Writers of America, the American Society for Psychical Research, the Magicians' Guild of America, the Magician's Club of London and other magical organizations.

MORRIS N. YOUNG, M.D., is a practicing ophthalmologist in New York City and holds degrees from M.I.T., Harvard and Columbia University College of Physicians and Surgeons. In addition to his professional memberships, he is a member of the Society of American Magicians. International Brotherhood of Magicians. The Magic Circle (London) and the Magic Collectors Association and he is founder and past editor of its publication, *Magicol.* With his wife, Chesley V. Young, he has established the largest private holding on Mnemonics. In 1955, with the late John J. McManus, the Youngs donated 20,000 items of magic and related fields material to the Library of Congress for joining with the Houdini Collection. Other McManus-Young collections have been established at the Library of the University of Texas, and the Library of the University of California in Berkeley. Dr. Young's published works on magic include *Hobby Magic,* and with Walter Gibson, *Houdini on Magic,* as well as many articles of historical interest in conjuring periodicals.

Vine Leaves Press

Enjoyed this book?
Go to *vineleavespress.com* to find more.
Subscribe to our newsletter:

Lightning Source UK Ltd.
Milton Keynes UK
UKHW040836180123
415545UK00005B/832